DEEP WATER, ANCIENT SHIPS

By Willard Bascom

DEEP WATER, ANCIENT SHIPS

WAVES AND BEACHES

HOLE IN THE BOTTOM OF THE SEA

GREAT SEA POETRY

*The Treasure Vault
of the Mediterranean*

~~~~~~~~~~~~~~~~~~~~~~~~~~~~~~~~~~~~~

DEEP WATER, ANCIENT SHIPS

WILLARD BASCOM

ILLUSTRATED BY THE AUTHOR

DOUBLEDAY & COMPANY, INC.
GARDEN CITY, NEW YORK
1976

Library of Congress Cataloging in Publication Data

Bascom, Willard.
Deep water, ancient ships.

Bibliography: p. 214
Includes index.
1. Mediterranean region—Antiquities. 2. Shipwrecks—Mediterranean Sea.
3. Shipwrecks—Black Sea. 4. Underwater archaeology. I. Title.
DE61.N3B37   930′.1′02804
ISBN 0-385-08982-1
Library of Congress Catalog Card Number 74–2503

For Rhoda
Friend and fellow adventurer

ACKNOWLEDGMENTS

In the preparation of this book I have been assisted by a number of people to whom I would like to express my most sincere appreciation:

My wife, Rhoda, who typed and retyped, criticized, and contributed many ideas. Virginia Mardesich, Rodney Wirtz, and Robin Simpson, who reviewed drafts and made helpful suggestions; Ms. Simpson also assisted with the final drawings. Dr. A. R. "Rocky" Miller of the Woods Hole Oceanographic Institution, who supplied data on the depths of the Mediterranean. Jim Dawson of Lloyd's of London, who did a great deal of digging in the archives of that remarkable institution and whose devastating views on the entrenched marine establishment buoyed my spirits. And all those good friends who did not come or call nights and weekends for a year while I lived in the ancient world.

I hope that the many persons whose writings and data I have used will feel generously dealt with in the credits that accompany the text. As with any new endeavor, it is necessary to build on the works of many who have gone before. They did wonderful work and I appreciate it all.

Contents

ILLUSTRATIONS

TABLES

DEEP WATER, ANCIENT SHIPS

Prologue

Somewhere, far out beneath the wine-dark sea of Ulysses, there lies an ancient wooden ship. It sits upright on the bottom, lightly covered by the sea dust of twenty-five hundred years. The wave-smashed deckhouse and splintered bulwarks tell of the violence of its last struggle with the sea. A stub of mast still remains, but the tattered sails and frayed cordage decayed into dust before the first Crusade. A few ballast stones leak from the hole where a weak plank finally gave way to let in the sea and bring about the end. But the cargo and its containers, the weapons and tools, and the personal possessions of the crew are still intact, neatly packaged in the wrecked hulk.

This ship is very old. It has waited since long before the time of Christ in the quiet and blackness of the abyss. It sails unmoving down the fourth dimension to meet us at some point in destiny, bearing evidence of a culture unknown to any living man. The ship was there when imperial Rome's galleys controlled the seas, when the forces of Christendom battled the infidels hundreds of fathoms above, when the pirates of Tripoli were stilled, and when Nazi submarines roamed unchecked.

Now the long, cold night is almost over. Soon a beam of sound will reveal the presence of this long-unseen vessel, and a ray of light will illuminate it for a television camera. We are approaching the moment when this ship and its treasure of ordinary articles will rise again to be appreciated by scholars and honored by the public.

Why did this ship survive when a million other sunken ships have reverted to dust so fine that it hangs like smoke in the sea? How would one go about seeking such a ship on the vastness of the sea bottom and recovering its historic treasures? Those questions are answered in this book.

When modern methods for studying the history of civilization as it is contained in deep and ancient ships are brought to bear, the result will be an understanding of events in man's early history that are not discoverable by any other means. They will supplement the excellent work done by classical researchers, archaeologists ashore, and shallow-water sea-diggers.

This new subscience is deepwater archaeology. It will be used to unlock the treasure vault of the ancient world.

CHAPTER I

Deep Ships, Ancient Treasure

This is a book about why ancient ships sank in deep water and how to find and salvage them. Its theme is that many of these ships and their cargoes remain in good condition because when they sank they came to rest in the special protective environment of the deep. There the old ships have been saved from waves and divers by great depth, from marine borers by a mud covering, and from chemical change by low levels of dissolved oxygen and low water temperatures. Certainly they are better preserved than their fellow ships that were wrecked in shallow water. With modern technology it is possible to find ancient wrecks in deep water, inspect them carefully, salvage historically or artistically valuable pieces, and recover entire ships.

Obviously, the searcher for ancient ships must look in the part of the world where ancient peoples traveled mainly by sea. Since the Mediterranean seas and the Black Sea meet that condition, this book is concerned with those waters. Ancient, for the purposes of discussion here, means before the time of Christ, and deep water means depths of greater than convenient diver depth, or from a hundred meters (about three hundred feet) down to the greatest depths of those seas.

The deep explorer-archaeologist is in pursuit of a dream that is

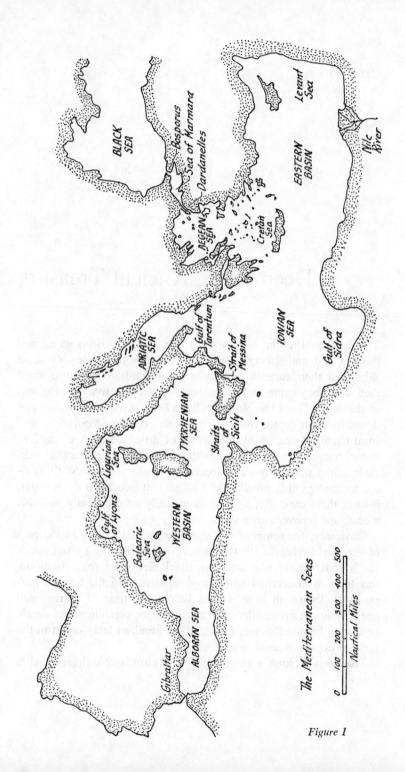

The Mediterranean Seas

Figure 1

generated by one tantalizing statistic: *One tenth of all the ships that have ever been built are on the bottom in deep water.*

This suggests a great level plain of gray ooze stretching off through blue haze into abyssal night. A submarine landscape populated with old hulks. But probably such a sight does not exist, for although the number of sunken ships down in deep water in the Mediterranean is very large (perhaps one hundred thousand ships of all ages), the area of deepwater bottom is even more impressive (about two and a half million square miles). Thus, the average population density of shipwrecks is only about one in every twenty-five square miles. Considering that a hull may not have survived boring animals, that it may be obscured by a thick cover of sediments, or that it may have landed on a bottom so complex that the searching instruments cannot separate it from the background, one might think that the chances of a successful search are too small to be worth a try.

Not so! Rather, the statistics make it clear that the archaeologist must optimize his chance of success by preparing a carefully thought-out strategy.

The bottom area to be considered can be greatly reduced if the searcher looks along the heavily traveled trade routes and at the sites of great naval battles. An area of perhaps 120,000 square miles probably contains most of the hulks of the estimated thirty thousand ships that went down offshore in ancient times. These bring the odds against the searcher down to about one ancient ship in four square miles.

The strategy can further be improved by taking other factors into account. For example, some parts of the sea were more dangerous than others; there are places where violent winds would suddenly arise and blow a ship over, and narrow passes between islands where pirates were likely to have attacked.

Searching is not equally easy everywhere, and a good knowledge of oceanography can improve the chances of detecting a wreck on the bottom and of finding an area where the wooden parts are most likely to have survived. A search will be easier if the bottom is smooth at a moderate depth, with a low sedimentation rate, low currents, and extremely clear water. The wood of the hull will be in the best condition if there is a low level of dissolved oxygen in the near-bottom water and no marine borers are present.

After carefully considering these matters and many others, search sites can be chosen where the chances of finding a well-preserved wreck on an uncluttered bottom with convenient working conditions are quite good.

Now the legal and political questions come into play. Many deepwater sites are beyond the twelve-mile limit claimed by most powers and thus are legally outside the jurisdiction of any country. However, the laws about the ownership of objects in the oceans are in the process of being changed. Although most of the international arguments are over natural resources rather than over salvageable property, feelings can run high and, in the absence of clear laws, the right to conduct archaeological operations will doubtless be governed by a local political decision. Even if the area chosen is on the "high seas," the salvage ship must have an operating port somewhere so it can provision and refuel and the crew can occasionally go ashore. This means the expedition must have tacit permission of that country or there will be problems of customs and taxes on any objects found and brought in on the ship.

The technical problems of how to go about finding, uncovering, inspecting, mapping, and carefully salvaging an ancient wreck are of most immediate concern. Obviously, there is no use in worrying about the other matters if there are no methods available for carrying out the work. But now the deep explorer can draw on recent advances in precise navigation devices, scanning sonars, and remote manipulators guided by high-quality television. Such equipment, mounted on the right sort of ship and manned by experienced technicians, can be used to conduct successful search and recovery operations. Thus, a great opportunity is presented to the archaeologist who wants to recover ancient artifacts from the previously unexplored deepwater domain. A new avenue for research into man's past is now open.

The proper way to begin any project is to make a list of objectives. In preparing to search the unexplored depths for treasures on ancient ships, one should say what one hopes to achieve and what treasures might be found.

The objectives of this book are to explain why the deep waters of the Mediterranean and Black seas are an excellent place to look for ancient ships in good condition, and to describe how the ships can be found and salvaged. The book will also discuss what ancient ships were like, where they voyaged, why they sank, and how the new findings will contribute to our knowledge of history.

The objectives of the expeditions that will follow this line of reasoning will be to

1. find, inspect, and map a number of ancient wrecks in deep water, amid reducing environments as well as in more normal conditions;
2. recover archaeologically important objects from these wrecks that will permit the date, national origin, ship type, and cargo to be identified;
3. salvage one or more selected wrecks by carefully bringing up part or all of the hull and cargo as indicated by the circumstances;
4. interpret the findings in the light of over-all knowledge of history and archaeology and publish the results in the scientific literature;
5. contribute the items recovered, along with the necessary documentation, to appropriate museums.

Other kinds of objectives develop as one proceeds to plan the central ones. For example, one would prefer to find wrecks from periods and nations about which little is known. Nearly any B.C. wreck will contain new information about the life and times when it sailed. But wrecks older than about 500 B.C. would be of special interest. Every historian would love to have new data on the Phoenicians, Minoans, or Mycenaeans, all of whom are believed to have traveled widely although little evidence has been found to date. Not much is known about the peoples who lived around the Black Sea, although their civilization in 1000 B.C. was probably equivalent to that in the Aegean. An early ship from the Crimea or Anatolia or Bulgaria would be a great find. The discovery of a warship, especially of "Sea Peoples" or Egyptian origin would be an archaeological milestone.

These subobjectives mean that priorities will be set that will influence the areas to be searched, the levels of effort to be applied to evaluating various hulks found, and the choice of ships to be eventually salvaged. All ancient wrecks are not of equal value. The rarest and best-preserved, in the most convenient areas, will get the most attention.

Treasure, like art, is in the eye of the beholder. It depends very largely on one's personal tastes and interests. Undersea finds that may be of great value to one person are quite worthless to another. For example: A bit of plant life, a shipwright's marking on a plank, a common cooking pot, or a roof tile may have great value to some archaeological scientist. Persons interested in art are anxious to see more of the great statuary from the golden age of Greece. Those probing ancient military affairs hope for new finds of armor and arms, as well as evidence about how galleys were rowed and how sea battles were fought. Anthropologists seek evidence about how ancient peoples lived and what cargoes were carried along the old trade routes. Historians want new written material—signed, dated, and carved in stone. Naval-architecture buffs are most interested in ship construction; they want to know what kind of wood each ship was built of and how it was assembled. A carbon 14 dating expert will be delighted with remnants of a half-eaten meal, a bit of charcoal, or a fragment of cloth. Museum directors may prefer items that can be spectacularly displayed and are of general public interest, such as jewelry, coins, carved sarcophagi, ship beaks, painted pottery, and helmets. Experts on science history would like to find mechanisms that show the levels of technology at various times in the past.

The archaeologist values them all. In the case of a deep complete wreck in one neat pile on the bottom, much of the value will come from the fact that the historic importance of each piece reinforces that of the others. The value of the whole is much greater than the sum of its parts, because it gives a short bright glimpse of a moment in history—a date when specific people were together on a purposeful voyage.

Practically everything that was used in the ancient world might be found on a sunken ship, and just about everything from the ancient world is now valuable to someone. Even pieces that contribute nothing new to our knowledge of history can be exceedingly valuable to people who want to touch the past vicariously through some artifact. They want to marvel at the mass-produced Scythian arrowhead and imagine it piercing a warrior's naked chest. They want to feel the cool gloom of an Egyptian tomb by fondling a scarab or a figurine. They want to hear the gurgle of wine poured when they touch an amphora. In this way, the past becomes close and real. To all these feelings, add the romance of an undersea burial of two thousand years' duration. Above these old wrecks navies fought, crusaders and saints voyaged, adventurers sailed. Now all these ancient objects, however insignificant originally or how modest in intrinsic value, are touched by the indefinable magic of forgotten centuries. A trace of ancestor worship, a bit of curiosity about the persons who once owned them, a snip of wonder that they have survived, all help make up the curious chemistry that attracts people to antiquities. Probably few people know even their own reasons for this urge to touch the past, but there is some of it in all of us.

In my living room is an amphora from a first-century-B.C. shipwreck. It was once a cheap, all-purpose container of smooth, pink clay. But two thousand years under water darkened it while bryozoans and calcareous worm tubes roughened its surface. Visitors are openly awed by the thought that some ancient mariner actually waded into the shallows with this specific container of wine in his arms. They see him pass it up to a friend on board, and they speculate on why amphorae are made in what appears at first to be a very inconvenient shape. Some are also impressed by the possibility that the worm tubes on it may be over a thousand years old. They touch it gently; then they think, visibly, of the world of twenty centuries ago that treated this "treasure" as we would a milk carton or a tin can.

In addition to the ship and its parts, every object and utensil, every material used in peace or war, every kind of art and architectural material, were moved about by ship and may possibly be brought up from deep water. Table 1 lists over a hundred objects that would be likely to have survived two thousand years beneath the sea.

Table 1. **Treasures That Might Be Found on Ancient Ships**

amphorae	fans	masks	sealing wax
amulets	fibulae	medallions	shields
anchors	figureheads	medical and	signets
arrowheads	figurines	musical	spears and spear
axes	fire pots	instruments	throwers
ballast	fishhooks	mirrors	statues
bas-reliefs	glassware	mosaics	steles
beads	grave slabs	mummies	swords
bells	grinding stones	necklaces	tablets
bowls	grommets	obelisks	tableware
bracelets	hammers	pendants	tiles
buckets	handles	pins	tools
caldrons	headdresses	pipes	tubes
carvings	helmets	plates	urns
chains	hoes	points	utensils
chariots	horns	pots	vases
coins	idols	querns	wax
columns	incense	ramming beaks	weapons
combs	ingots	ravens	whetstones
cups	inlaid objects	razors	and perhaps
daggers	jars	rhyta	items connected
disks	knives	sarcophagi	with Xerxes and
enamelware	lamps	scarabs	Zoroaster
eyes (of ships)	lunulae	seals and	

The above objects may be made of the following materials which will survive two thousand years under the sea: Rock—diorite, granite, jade, lapis
lazuli, limestone, marble, obsidian. Metal—bronze, gold, lead, possibly
silver and iron. Man-made—ceramics, faience, glass.

Amid special chemical conditions, nearly anything might survive for thousands of years beneath the sea. But exactly the right
conditions are rare; ordinarily only a few materials have an excellent chance of surviving without degradation. These are natural rocks such as diorite, granite, obsidian, or marble, and gem
minerals; some metals, especially gold, lead, and bronze; and ceramic materials and glass.

The survival of other materials depends on the condition of
burial at the sea floor. Generally, massive pieces can be expected
to survive better than thin, delicate ones. Most iron, silver, and

copper items will probably have disappeared. Limestone objects, which are attacked by marine borers in shallow water, will probably survive at depth. Some glass and faience pieces will be in excellent condition, but others will have spalled to dust, depending on the mix of materials and the conditions in the kiln.

In many cases the organic materials, including the wood of the hull, will have completely disappeared. Only the hard, sea-resistant pieces remain, forming a low, silt-covered mound.

Wooden shipwrecks and their cargoes disintegrate because of a complex combination of physical, chemical, and biological factors. Although deep water reduces the speed of the destruction, it does not eliminate it completely. There is very little physical damage after the ship reaches the bottom. The orbital motions of waves that create violent to-and-fro motions of the water near the bottom in shallow depths decrease to zero in depths of over a hundred meters. This means that there is no strain on the hull planking and no abrasion caused by sand in moving water. Generally, the currents in the deep are too slow to shift the wreckage or scatter evidence. The weight of the slowly accumulating silt is not likely to collapse the remaining hull.

Water pressure becomes greater with depth because of the increasing weight of the water above, the increase being about .74 kilogram per square centimeter for each meter of depth (or one pound per square inch for every two feet of depth). However, the effects of pressure on most objects are insignificant, since most materials are only slightly compressible. Only if there is an enclosed air space, such as might exist in a sealed space or an amphora not quite full of oil or wine, can pressure cause damage. Wood would become waterlogged, which simply means that the tiny air spaces between the fibers are flooded, but the shape of the ship parts would not change.

The chemistry of deep Mediterranean waters, although not very different from that near the surface, is somewhat more favorable to wreck survival; the bottom water is a little cooler and a little less salty. Salt water is a decidedly corrosive medium, and even a slight decrease in salinity will tend to reduce the disintegration of metals. Temperature is more important; the bottom waters of the Mediterranean average about 13° Celsius (55° Fahrenheit),

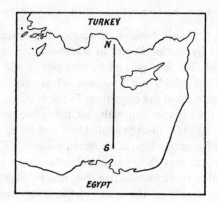

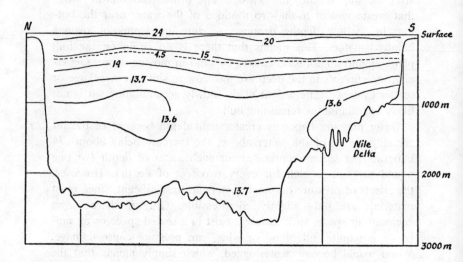

Temperature and Depth in
the Eastern Basin
100:1 vert. exag.

After Mediterranean Sea Atlas

which is about 10° cooler than the average surface temperatures (but notably warmer than the water at the bottom of the oceans, which is around 4° C). Since each decrease of 10° halves the speed of a chemical reaction, degradation in the deep is only about half as fast as in shallow water. Biological processes, which are a more complicated form of chemistry, are similarly slowed.

Another very important factor in deep-wreck survival is the amount of dissolved oxygen in the water. Most sea animals do very well if there is more than four parts per million of dissolved oxygen in sea water; below that amount their numbers generally decrease and, as the dissolved oxygen approaches zero, the bottom becomes a world of almost-death. This means that sea borers cannot live and that no animals disturb the bottom mud. If the bottom contains a great excess of organic material that immediately uses up any new oxygen that appears, a reducing environment is said to exist. Sulphides form, including the deadly and foul-smelling hydrogen sulphide gas (H_2S), and only anaerobic bacteria can live. Dark bottom muds accumulate to form strata that are undisturbed by sea life and so retain precise yearly layers that can be counted.

These areas of the sea floor where death pervades are of intense interest to the deepwater archaeologist. In these reducing environments, organic substances such as wood, rigging, foodstuffs, and corpses may survive completely. With no borers, no scavengers, and only anaerobic bacteria, one can hope that ancient soft objects can be retrieved in their entirety, looking much as they did on the day they sank. In such areas, there is a chance of making a

Figure 2. **Temperature and Depth in the Eastern Basin**
   The oceanographer diagnoses the character of a sea by its depth, temperature, and oxygen supply. Much of the eastern Mediterranean is over two thousand meters deep, except where the Nile has deposited thick muds near the southern shore. Temperatures at both bottom and surface are warm even in the winter months. The dashed line shows the upper boundary of water with 4.5 parts per million of dissolved oxygen—ample to sustain sea life.

major break-through in marine archaeology. Such a find will be the marine equivalent of the beautifully preserved corpses from the Danish bogs that look as good as new after two thousand years. The entire deep Black Sea floor has reducing conditions, and scientists have already found delicate biological membranes seventy thousand years old in the sediments there.

Even in the usual, oxidizing conditions, the impact of a sinking ship landing on a soft mud bottom will throw much mud into suspension that will slowly settle back to form a protective covering. If it covers the "substrate," as biologists call surfaces that look delectable to borer larvae, even a very thin layer of mud may be protective.

Ceramic objects, especially pottery made of fired clay, will remain virtually unchanged for thousands of years. The evidence on this is quite clear, since piles of amphorae are the most distinguishing feature of most wrecks. Many thousands of amphorae have already been brought up in virtually new condition. Objects made of ceramics also include tiles for fireplaces and roofs, plates and jugs, and decorated tablets. It is also possible that some of the high-quality black and red figured vases from classical Greece or the eggshell ware of Crete will be found in a wreck. But most of the pottery finds will be the commonly carried amphorae. It is rather hard to imagine an old wreck without amphorae, since they were generally used as shipboard containers for water and foodstuffs for several thousand years.

Objects made of glass might be found on ships wrecked after about 800 B.C., when glassmaking furnaces first came into use. Before that time, a glasslike material of brilliant blue called faience was made by adding copper minerals to quartz sand and sodium carbonate (at lower temperatures than those for glassmaking). Egyptian blue faience beads were widely traded throughout the Mediterranean by 4000 B.C., and samples found on one ancient ship were undamaged from being two thousand years under water. Natural volcanic glass (obsidian), used by Neolithic man for arrowheads, was another early article of trade. Since the volcano of its origin can be identified and since later peoples made sophisticated household articles from it, obsidian objects are particularly valuable to the archaeologist.

Semiprecious stones such as chalcedony, steatite, and lapis lazuli were often carved into signet rings and cylinder seals. These small works of art, representing animals, kings hunting, or warships, were used as a signature or identification to make impressions on soft wax or clay. Since the owner always carried his seal with him, there is a very good chance of finding seals on a wreck.

Table 2. **Statue Finds in the Mediterranean Sea. Bronzes from the Fifth to First Centuries B.C.**

Date Found	Location	Subject
1700?	"Found in the Sea"	Homer or Sophocles
1809	Gulf of Corinth, Greece	Zeus
1832	Piombino, Tuscany, Italy	Apollo
1837	Skiathos, Greece	A god
1901	Antikythera, Greece	Philosopher, Athlete
1907–13	Mahdia, Tunis	Aphrodite, Dionysus, Aesculapus, Athena, Hygeia, Eros, Artemis
1925	Bay of Marathon, Greece	Youth
1928	Cape Artemision, Greece	Poseidon, Jockey Boy
1929	Rhodes, Greece	Aphrodite
1953	Marmaris, Turkey	Demeter
1960	Shirki Rocks, Sicily	Bronze statue
1962	Anatolia, Turkey	Negro boy, Fortuna statuette

Gold is likely to be found on a wreck in the form of jewelry and coins. This will not be treasure in the usual sense, because the archaeological and historical values will far outweigh the intrinsic value; however, its presence on a wreck even in small quantities is very likely to start rumors and cause special customs problems. Gold is valuable partly because it is impervious to degradation; objects made of it will be absolutely unchanged.

Lead objects such as sounding weights, piping, and anchors will also remain whole, but the metal of greatest interest is bronze. Bronze came into general use about 2000 B.C., when it was discovered that a mixture of about seven parts copper and one part tin formed a new metal with greatly superior properties. It was first used for weapons, but in time jewelry, coins, household articles, and objects of art were made of it. Because bronze is so resistant to corrosion in sea water, some wonderful statues from the classical age of Greece have survived two thousand years of immersion to demonstrate the artistic accomplishments of the Greeks. In fact, much early marine archaeology was directed toward recovering the great statues named in Table 2. With luck, more may be found in deep water.

On rare occasions, some object is discovered that suddenly illuminates the technology of the ancient world and gives us new insight into archaeological possibilities. One example of such a treasure is the computer of Antikythera.

When the famous wreck of Antikythera was salvaged in 1901, a scholarly dispute arose over the time when the wreck occurred. This was because the bronze statues were from the fourth century B.C., the marble statues seemed to be copies made in a later period, and some pottery shards were dated first century B.C.

Some years later, a young Greek archaeologist, sorting through miscellaneous unidentified objects from the wreck, came across what looked to him like a clockwork mechanism made of bronze and inscribed with ancient Greek astronomical symbols. Those who saw it thought it might be an early astrolabe or some kind of navigational instrument. Others felt it was far too complex a device for the B.C. period and thought perhaps it had been accidentally dropped on the site a thousand years later. Nearly everyone realized it was both important and unique, so it was set aside for later study.

Fifty years later, Dr. Derek de Solla Price, a physicist interested in the history of science, obtained a grant from the American Philosophical Society to go to Athens and study the device. He described it as "a box with dials on the outside and a very complex assembly of gear wheels mounted within, probably resembling a well-made 18th century clock." Doors hinged to the box served to protect the dials, and on them, as well as on all other available surfaces, there were long Greek inscriptions describing the construction and operation of the instrument.

The front dial showed the motions of the sun in the zodiac as well as the rising of bright stars and constellations throughout the year. The back dial seemed to have kept track of the phases of the moon and the positions of the planets. A slip ring on the front dial was provided for adjustment, because the old Egyptian calendar, on which the instrument was based, had no leap year and so lost one quarter day each year.

When they dried out, the wooden parts shrank and fell apart so that much of the detailed information from the inscriptions was lost. However, at least twenty gear wheels, all made of a low-tin bronze, were well preserved, including a very sophisticated assembly of gears that probably functioned as a differential gear system. The input was through an axle, probably rotated by hand, that turned two trains of gears and, eventually, pointers on the dials. Thus, when the main axle was turned, all the pointers turned simultaneously at various speeds.

This mechanism must have worked, because it was mended twice; we can assume it was in use when the wreck occurred. The two scales are set in such a way as to be out of phase by 13.5°—a circumstance that could occur only at 80 B.C. (or 200 B.C. or A.D. 40). But a fiducial mark indicates it was "set" for 82 B.C., which must have been the year of the wreck.

The Greek word forms used were much like those of another inscription, written by Geminos of Rhodes in 77 B.C., and thus the mechanism is tentatively credited to him. Nothing like this remarkable instrument is preserved elsewhere. Although its authenticity is now unquestioned, there are no scientific or literary allusions to anything comparable, and the closest known similar mechanism is a thirteenth-century Islamic calendar computer.

In summary, there are many kinds of ancient treasures in the sea, ranging from soft objects in reducing environments and articles of common use to complex clockwork mechanisms and great art.

One begins the search by learning about the seas that hold the treasure. With persistence and the best of modern undersea technology, they can be explored and treasures brought up that will increase our knowledge of ancient peoples.

CHAPTER II

The Mediterranean and Black Seas

The seas that are the setting for the proposed exploration are large, with complicated shore lines and undersea topography. Decisions on where and how to search the depths for ancient wrecks require a knowledge of geography, meteorology, and oceanography.

The Mediterranean is literally a sea amid lands, whose great embayments are seas in their own right. It has long been both a barrier and a route for contacts between the peoples on opposite sides. By trial and error, the early peoples discovered how to build ships and how to sail them between ports through a complex maze of islands, making use of winds that changed direction and velocity from morning to night and from season to season. The search for new insights into the civilizations of those ancient mariners is the objective of this research.

A series of hollows between Europe and Africa rimmed with dry, rugged lands and filled with water make up the Mediterranean seas: Alborán, Balearic, Ligurian, Tyrrhenian, Ionian, Adriatic, Aegean, Cretan, and Levant. All are part of, or are connected to, two great basins that lie along an east-west crack in the earth's structure where the continents, once joined, have now parted. Two bridges of continental rocks remain, thinly covered

Ancient Greece

0   50   100
Nautical Miles

with water, to tie the land masses together—at the Straits of Sicily and the Strait of Gibraltar.

Along the rims of the two basins, the civilizations of the ancient world arose. All the coast lines are irregular, but the Greek-Turkish archipelago is especially so, being a drowned mountain range whose tops form islands and whose elongated ridges are finger-like peninsulas.

In an area of islands, mountainous back country, and desert conditions along many coasts, all of which might possibly contain hostile tribes, people found it practical to move about by sea. The invention of some form of boat capable of crossing straits or water between islands that are visible one from another must have come far back in man's history, possibly ten thousand years ago or more. The direct evidence for movement of pottery by boats goes back at least six thousand years, and it is not likely this was the actual beginning.

The Mediterranean has a surface area of 2.96 million square kilometers and a volume of 4.24 million cubic kilometers. Its main basins are as deep as the oceans, the western one having a flat floor about twenty-seven hundred meters (8,856 feet) deep, the eastern basin being about the same average depth but not so flat. The deepest spots are southeast of Rhodes, where an area of about one thousand square miles is deeper than four thousand meters. (For a reasonable approximation, multiply meters by three to convert to feet. Also see Appendix 2 for metric conversion factors.) Southwest of the Peloponnesus, an area of about the same size contains the maximum depth of 4,982 meters (16,341 feet). The Ionian Sea is both broad and deep, with nearly a hundred thousand square miles deeper than three thousand

Figure 3. **Ancient Greece**

The shore lines of the Aegean and Cretan seas are very complicated. Principal ship routes such as those from Piraeus or Chios to Rhodes went through many dangerous passes between islands where a ship could easily be caught by a storm and driven ashore or overwhelmed as it tried to fight its way to open water. Therefore these seas are excellent hunting grounds for ancient wrecks.

meters. The shallow areas are the Aegean, the Adriatic, and a huge area south and west of Sicily where there is very little water deeper than five hundred meters.

Shallow, of course, means shallow to an oceanographer or to a deep water salvage man, not to a diver. There are over a hundred thousand square miles of the Mediterranean that are between a hundred and five hundred meters (three hundred to fifteen hundred feet) where ancient ships might well be found and in which there are excellent target areas.

The kind of material on the bottom falls into two main classes: calcareous muds or clays, and sand or rock. The former predominates over 90 per cent of the Mediterranean where deep-sea conditions prevail, while the rocky and sandy areas are more characteristic of the Aegean and other areas near shores with steep hills and high erosion rates. Generally the sedimentation in the deep basins is slow, being mainly a combination of wind-blown dust and the shells of tiny calcareous animals. On the average, about twenty centimeters (eight inches) of sediment has been added to the deep bottom since the beginning of our calendar.

The level of the sea relative to the adjacent land is changing in a number of places. Slow tectonic movements in the earth's crust have adjusted the elevation of many ancient coastal towns upward or downward at rates of about one meter per thousand years, so that some are now inland and others are submerged. These deep geological processes are abetted by surface ones: erosion of the fine materials from the hillsides after the removal of trees in ancient times, soil losses from lowlands as the combined result of plowing and flooding, and siltation in bays. Also, volcanoes have suddenly belched out new islands and exploded to destroy old ones. All these natural forces are steadily changing the shore line.

The Mediterranean is a sea full of islands. Nearly everyone is familiar with the large ones: Sicily, Corsica, Sardinia, Crete, and Cyprus. But there are some fascinating smaller ones that also have an illustrious history. The names are well known, but not many people know where Ibiza, Elba, Ithaca, Malta, Rhodes, Thera, and Lesbos are located. There are hundreds more, each of which hoards some bit of ancient history in a cave or cove or ruin and which may well have ancient ships down offshore.

In discussing the Mediterranean, it is not long before the subject of the eruption of Santorin comes up. The explosion of this great volcano in about 1500 B.C. changed the course of human history by destroying a major center of culture. Before this great eruption, the island of Thera must have been mainly a single volcanic mountain. It was a garden spot, because things grew so well on the rich, volcanic soil. Living was easy; the Minoan fleet gave protection from attack and the people had leisure time for attention to such gentle arts as fresco painting.

Then came the disaster that is often compared with the eruption of Krakatoa in the Dutch East Indies. The report of the Royal Society of London on that eruption contained some dramatic eyewitness descriptions of Krakatoa. Think of Santorin while reading the following account:

In 1883 the volcano Krakatoa in the Sunda Straits, Dutch East Indies, erupted for four days with the most violent explosions of recorded history. The entire northern portion of the island disappeared and in place of ten square miles of land with an average elevation of 700 feet, there was formed a great depression with its bottom more than 900 feet below sea level.

It is estimated that four and one-eighth cubic miles of rock was blown away by subsequent explosions. The sea was covered with masses of pumice for miles around and in many places it was so thick that no vessel could force its way through. Two new islands rose in the Sunda Straits and obstructed the principal ship channels; the lighthouses were swept away; all the old familiar landmarks were obscured by a vast deposit of volcanic dust and the sea bottom became covered with a thick layer of rock debris.

The most damaging effect of the eruption was the initiation of seismic sea waves which inundated the whole of the fore-shores of Java and Sumatra bordering the Strait. Three villages were carried away by water which reached heights of 60 to 115 feet. More than 36,000 people were drowned and many vessels were washed ashore including a government steamer which was carried 1.8 miles inland and left 32 feet above sea level.

The eruption of Santorin was substantially larger than that of Krakatoa, with estimates ranging up to four times the explosive force. The caldera at Santorin is said to be five times larger, and quarry excavations have disclosed that the ash blanket on Thera is much deeper than that left around Krakatoa. If one takes the well-documented tales of Krakatoa and translates them thirty-four hundred years backward in time, one can imagine the destruction that took place around the Cretan Sea. The cities of Thera had apparently been evacuated, since no bodies or valuables have been found in the buildings, but some ships of the fleeing refugees must have been sunk by volcanic bombs, others by waves from the blast. Both these events may be helpful to the deepwater archaeologist. The volcanic ash from that dated eruption will be visible in cores of Aegean sediments, and one can directly measure the thickness of sediment above it to determine the sedimentation rate. Ships sunk directly or sucked back offshore by the runoff from waves striking the Cretan shore may be a valuable objective, since little is known about Minoan ships.

The tsunami (tidal wave) created by the explosion would have crossed the seventy-five-mile-wide Cretan Sea in 22½ minutes at two hundred miles per hour. On moving into shallow water, it would have formed huge, breaking waves (the height depending on the underwater configuration) that would have wrought tremendous destruction on all ports, coastal cities, and ships on the north side of the Minoan island. The run-up (distance the water moved inland) was probably not great, perhaps a few miles in low valleys, but it seems to have been sufficient to destroy the essence of Minoan civilization. The ancient world changed with a single blast, and it was many years before their high standards of living were achieved again.

Santorin is not quite dead; it has erupted at least once in the intervening years and may go off again someday. At present, the only sign of activity is some hot springs that bubble from a small crater off the island of Thera accompanied by sulphurous fumes. The local fishing boats come there periodically to spend a few leisurely days moored to the rocks while the toxic water kills the weed on their hulls and the borers in them. Then, with clean bottoms, they go back to work.

Generally, the water of the Mediterranean seas is very clear and very blue. It is so clear that a diver can often see thirty meters and sometimes fifty or more. The sea dust, on being stirred, settles

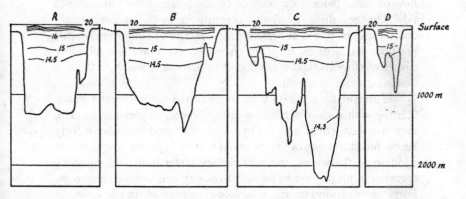

Temperature and Depth in the Sea of Crete and Approaches 100:1 vert. exag.

After Mediterranean Sea Atlas

Figure 4. **Temperature and Depth in the Sea of Crete**

The characteristics of these moderately deep waters are fairly uniform and there is ample oxygen in the depths for all sea life. Legs B and C, whose apex is near Thera, undoubtedly have a bottom composed largely of volcanic ash under the more recent muds.

rapidly or slowly drifts away, leaving the diver suspended free in "space." Photos made by marine archaeologists of work on near-shore wrecks look much as though they were made through air instead of sea water. When viewed from a coastal cliff, the water is such an intense blue that it seems especially deep and mysterious, setting the observer dreaming of ancient ships and legends.

The tides in the Mediterranean are generally very small, rarely exceeding a few centimeters, so it is somewhat surprising that their cause was understood by the ancients. In the first century A.D., Pliny remarked on the wonderful circumstance of the ebb and flow of water twice a day caused by the sun and the moon. Since tidal changes drive the local currents in much of the world's coastal waters, one is at first surprised that the Mediterranean currents are as large as they are. Actually, there are several other causes of currents, and it is difficult to determine which of these is dominant at any moment.

The drag of the wind on the surface of the sea moves the water. Starting with a calm sea and a rising breeze, ripples are formed, then wavelets, chop, and finally, when the wind gets above forty knots, full storm waves five to seven meters high are generated. In addition to the waves, the near-surface water is moved along by the wind in proportion to the wind velocity and surface roughness. Forty knots of wind creates a surface current of about one knot.

The largest current-causing factor in the Mediterranean is evaporation. Winds dried by the deserts to the south evaporate fantastic quantities of water as they blow across the sea, taking with them about a thousand cubic miles of water a year or, on the average, eighty thousand tons a second.

This amount of water cannot be made up by the inflow from the Rhone, the Nile, and those rivers that overflow the Black Sea through the Turkish straits. Rather, the evaporation losses are constantly replaced from the Atlantic by an inflow through the Strait of Gibraltar. The surface water in the strait, which always moves eastward, flows at two to four knots, with an average volume of two million tons per second. This is far more than the amount evaporated; the difference is accounted for by an outflow beneath the surface through the strait. This countercurrent that flows westward is composed of much heavier, saltier water, so that the salinity in the Mediterranean does not increase but is constantly maintained at a somewhat higher level than the Atlantic. If it were not for this subsurface discharge, in a few years the evaporation would convert the Mediterranean into a huge dead sea.

The enclosed nature of the eastern basin is reflected in its higher salinity (thirty-nine parts per thousand) and higher surface temperature, which ranges from 17 to 24° C. In spite of constant replenishment through Gibraltar, the average water level in the Mediterranean remains some ten centimeters lower than the Atlantic in the winter and three times that much in the summer, when evaporation is higher.

In the western basin, the water is not only less saline than in the east, but is somewhat colder, the surface temperature being 13–14° C. As water evaporates from the surface, the remaining surface waters become saltier and heavier than those below. This unstable condition cannot exist for long, and from time to time the water structure abruptly collapses. Then the heavy water falls to the bottom, whence it moves westward, toward the outflow. The implication of these water motions is that oxygenated surface waters are carried to the bottom and that the larvae of marine borers are transplanted to deep wreck sites. Both are important to the deep archaeologist.

The somewhat swifter currents that exist in narrow passes where the water rushes through may prevent sedimentation and result in a clean, water-scoured bottom. Possibly in such places the hard parts and artifacts from ancient ships will lie nakedly exposed on the sea bottom.

In the Strait of Messina the currents are driven both by tidal forces and by saline differences. Every twelve hours, when the waters of the Tyrrhenian Sea and the Ionian Sea try to exchange, this produces currents of as much as four knots. At some times, there may be layers of water moving in opposite directions, producing shear and turbulence. According to Ernle Bradford, a well-known authority on such subjects, the whirlpool of Charybdis, well known to the fishermen of the adjacent Sicilian town of Ganzirri, results from this turbulence. On the opposite, Italian shore, their rivals from the village of Scilla, named after the monster of the Odyssey, say that on a gray day when the currents from the south buck the wind from the north, one can still hear Scylla's yelp as the wind and the sea boom against the rocks and cry in the caves.

Charybdis apparently is not as great a whirlpool as it once was, because of a change in the structure of the seabed caused by an earthquake in 1783. Even so, in sailing days a British admiral wrote that ". . . small craft are endangered by it and I have seen several men-of-war whirled round on its surface."

There are also notable currents in the Dardanelles, where the waters of the Sea of Marmara enter the Aegean. On the Asiatic side of the Dardanelles the current often flows at three knots, while close against the European side it is less than half that figure. A few miles upstream, in the one-mile-wide "narrows" (where Xerxes built his famous bridge of boats in 480 B.C.), the currents run evenly at about two knots, being unexpectedly higher near the banks than at the center. It was at this point that Lord Byron and a British naval officer swam across in imitation of Leander. Their crossing time was one hour and ten minutes, and the actual distance they covered was nearly four miles. When the north wind blows in reinforcement, this current can run as high as five knots. Other places where substantial currents may flow, and thus might influence archaeological exploration, include narrow passes between some of the Greek islands (especially east and west of Crete), the Straits of Sicily, and the strait between Sardinia and Corsica.

Mediterranean summers are sunny and warm, when the trade winds blow from the south; but the winter months, when the northerlies blow, are cold and damp. When the winter storms come, the blast of salt spray makes sailors uncomfortable and apprehensive. They reef the sails, pull their jackets tightly about themselves, and head for a safe anchorage.

In the western Mediterranean, when an atmospheric depression moves eastward across Spain and through the Strait of Gibraltar it causes strong northwest gales along the whole North African coast. An unwary mariner may find himself swept against a hostile lee shore; the whole coast from Tangier to Cape Bon is a graveyard of ships that were wrecked there from classical times up to the present. The Spaniards lost several fleets off Algeria during their conflict with the Moors in the sixteenth century. In 1541, one of the worst maritime disasters in history was brought about by a storm that struck just as the fleet of Emperor Charles V was poised to invade. Many galleys, as well as a hundred and fifty galleons carrying eight thousand troops and the flower of Spanish nobility, perished in what became known as "Charles's Gale." The emperor, contemplating the wreckage of his fleet and army, is said to have bowed his head and murmured, "Thy will be done."

The dreaded northerly winter wind that causes so much misery has been given a different name by each bordering country.

The mistral, as the winter wind that blows south across France is called, is cold, dry, and dusty. It arises from a high-pressure area in the Alps to the north and sends its cold draft down the sunny Rhone Valley. When the mistral collides with the warm sea breezes, the result is short, vicious storms that have sent many a luckless ship to the bottom.

The bora, a northern wind that blasts its way down the Adriatic between Italy and Croatia, rapidly reaches whole-gale strength and makes waves seven to ten meters high. Gusts reach over a hundred knots, and life lines are rigged along streets in Trieste to help pedestrians keep their footing. In Venetian times, ships from northern Adriatic ports were actually forbidden to return home in November to December because of the greatly increased chance of loss. A violent bora can arise very suddenly, and even large modern steel ships sometimes disappear with all hands.

Farther east, the same wind, now called the Greek wind, or gregale, blows south across the normally tranquil Ionian Sea from the mountains of Greece and Albania toward the shores of Africa.

Bad weather was the main cause of ships sinking in ancient times; in the early days of the struggle between Carthage and Rome, the latter lost four ships to the weather for every one lost in battle. There was a whimsical proverb of galley warfare in the Middle Ages that there were "four ports for a fleet: June, July, August, and Port Mahon." In 491 B.C., Darius lost a fleet to a storm at the tip of Mount Athos peninsula, which thwarted his attempt to invade Greece. In his preparations for the next war with Greece, he actually dug a canal one and a half miles long across

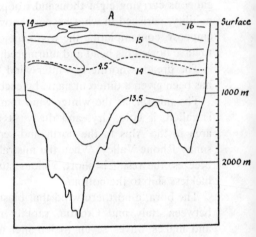

----- Dissolved oxygen, parts per million

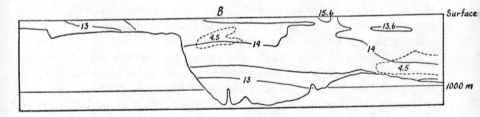

Temperature and Depth in
the Adriatic Sea and Across
Its Entrance
100:1 vert. exag.

After Mediterranean Sea Atlas

the base of the peninsula of Mount Athos, one of the fingers of Thrace, to avoid having his ships go around its stormy tip—a total sea distance of only sixty miles.

Unless the captain of a sailing ship has considerable local experience or employs a local pilot, his ship may be overwhelmed by downdrafts from the mountains as it passes them on their southern side. These downdrafts can increase a good, force-five sailing breeze to gale-force gusts. Areas where this phenomenon occurs include the southern coast of Crete (the Admiralty Pilot warns mariners to stay at least five miles out to sea), the eastern side of the Gulf of Athens, and the southern and eastern sides of the Cyclades.

The principal southern wind is the sirocco, also called simoom or khamsin. It is a hot wind loaded with dust it picks up in crossing the desert. This drying wind is said to "split furniture, crack the soul, and send sailors to the north again." A big sirocco can last a week, blowing a steady force six, gusting to eight or ten. In 1966, a large, modern Greek steamer, the M.S. *Heraklion* went down with 230 people in a sirocco—doubtless to a bottom littered with wrecks from ancient times.

One of the oceanographic survey ships that was responsible for making many of the deep "stations" that are presented in the Atlas of the Mediterranean was the auxiliary schooner *Atlantis* of the Woods Hole Oceanographic Institution. The following sentences, taken from the preface to that atlas, describe some of the things *Atlantis* learned about Mediterranean winds in addition to the data on salinity, temperature, and dissolved oxygen it was seeking:

Atlantis had considerable difficulty beginning her first section. A northern storm prevented her from leaving the North African

Figure 5. **Temperature and Depth in the Adriatic Sea**
The upper Adriatic is very shallow, but the southern end has water depths of about one thousand meters. This is the place where the deadly bora has sunk a great many ships, both ancient and modern, and where conditions for the survival of old hulls are good.

coast. For three successive nights the lights of the city of Algiers were in view in spite of all attempts to make sea room. . . . At first the Tyrrhenian section proceeded smoothly but as the weather worsened again all operations ceased and the ship had to run before a gale to seek shelter south of the Straits of Messina. . . . Work south and east of Rhodes was suspended because of storms. . . . The last station was made under full power against the wind as still another gale threatened to suspend operations.

In the Aegean and the Black seas the prevailing winds during the summer sailing season are from north to northwest. The ancient Greeks referred to them as "etesian," meaning that they are reliable and return every year. In the Aegean this wind is called the melteme. It begins, according to Herodotus, with the rising of the Dog Star in early July, and continues to the middle of September. On a typical melteme day in the Cyclades Isles it is calm at dawn but by full daylight a pleasant northerly breeze will have begun to ruffle the blue water. By afternoon the breeze can increase to 20–30 knots but it begins to drop as the sun sets, and at midnight the sea is calm again. Sometimes these afternoon winds reach gale velocities and raise waves four meters high; occasionally, they blow all night. As a result, the custom was to sail between harbors from dawn until early afternoon and then anchor until the following day.

It was on the etesian winds that early Greek trade depended. Running before them, the old ships could easily cross the Aegean, visit Crete and Rhodes, and sail on to Egypt. Returning home was more of a problem, but they could tack to take advantage of variations in the wind direction, or row, or wait for a more favorable season. As a result, the passage time in one direction often took far less time than if the same ship went the other way. The ancient freighters could "make good" about four to six knots while running before the wind, perhaps two knots against it. Trade between Egypt and Rhodes continued the year around but in much of the Aegean, trade simply stopped in October and ships were laid up until the following May.

In the spring, southwesterlies blowing in the Aegean made it possible for the ancient mariners to sail north through the Turkish straits. Currents in the straits may have forced the sailors to row part of the way through or even to tow their boats from the shore for short distances. But, once in the Black Sea, they could sail again.

Compared to the winds, other factors that controlled ship commerce were minor. Ancient trade moved with the wind, and in deference the Athenians built a tower that still stands below the Acropolis. At its top is a revolving Triton who points his staff in the direction of the wind. Below him on the marble sides of the octagonal structure are carved figures that symbolize each of the eight winds.

Prof. Lionel Casson, who has written extensively on ancient mariners, quotes the historian Vegetius, who says that the best parts of the sailing season are from 27 May to 14 September and that the absolute outside limits are 10 March to 10 November. During fall and winter, sailing was reduced to the absolute minimum; only vital dispatches, urgently needed supplies, and emergency military equipment moved by sea. Aside from ships transporting those necessities, the sea lanes were deserted— although in times when pirates were a serious menace the winter weather was a lesser risk. The problem of winter sailing was as much one of cloud cover as of storm. Mariners who sail without a compass must be able to see the sun and the stars or at least sight distant headlands to get their bearing. In winter, when days were short, skies cloudy, and stars obscured, ships could not be sure what direction they were going. Sailors refused to sail, insurance rates went up, and ship traffic came to a virtual standstill.

Northward from the Aegean Sea, the Turkish straits lead to the Black Sea. Amid that passage, between the Dardanelles and the Bosporus, is the Sea of Marmara. Not much is known about the depths of that small sea except that a few oceanographic stations made there by *Atlantis* show very little oxygen near the bottom in one of its deep areas. This suggests strongly that those deep puddles have reducing conditions at the bottom. Since this relatively restricted route has been well traveled for many thousands of years, it seems likely that old ships are down there. If so, some have landed in the bottoms of the anoxic basins. Thus a prime place to search for well-preserved wrecks is the basins of the Sea of Marmara.

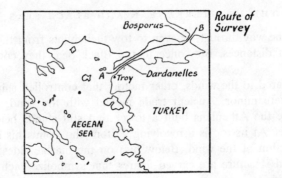

Route of
Survey

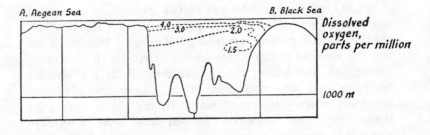

A. Aegean Sea   B. Black Sea

Dissolved
oxygen,
parts per million

1000 m

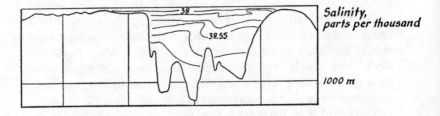

Salinity,
parts per thousand

1000 m

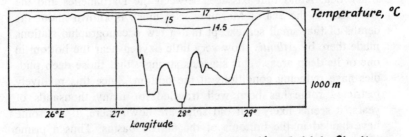

Temperature, °C

1000 m

26°E   27°   28°   29°
Longitude

Oceanographic Section Through the Turkish Straits
Showing the Deep Zone in the Sea of Marmara
Where Dissolved Oxygen Is Very Low

After Mediterranean Sea Atlas

The Black Sea is unique among all the world's seas because of its remarkable stratification into two distinct layers. The surface water is relatively fresh and light, since it comes from the great northern rivers: Don, Danube, and Dnieper. But below two hundred meters the water is salty, with a high density; very little mixing takes place. Even when the surface waters become very cold ($-1°$ C), they still are less dense than the deep water and do not sink.

It is the non-mixing that makes the Black Sea so special. The unchanging layers imply a barrier, and without some vertical motion of the water there is no mechanism to transport oxygen from the atmosphere to the bottom. No oxygen means that no fish or invertebrates can live there; the bottom layer of that sea has been poisoned by deadly hydrogen sulphide. With H_2S instead of oxygen, there can be no wood-devouring borers or scavengers and no microbial degradation of organic materials including ship hulls. Black sulphide compounds form; thus the name, Black Sea. But above, the well-oxygenated surface layer is much like a huge lake, with lots of fish and many summer resorts along the coast. In ancient times, Jason and his Argonauts explored its perimeter, the Trojans taxed the ships as they entered, and Greek city-states colonized its rim.

Many of the following data come from a review paper by the famous Russian oceanographer L. Zenkevich, who cites the work of his countrymen over the past century in exploring the Black Sea. This great inland sea is about the same latitude as the Great Lakes; its greatest length is 620 nautical miles, and its width at the center is about 210 nautical miles. The average depth is 1,271 meters, the greatest depth 2,247 meters. The average annual river inflow of fresh water is four hundred cubic kilometers, while two hundred cubic kilometers of saline waters enter from the Sea of Marmara to the south in an exchange similar to that at Gibraltar.

Figure 6. **Oceanographic Section Through the Turkish Straits**
The deep hole in the heavily traveled Sea of Marmara is one of the best places to search for ancient ships. Its high salinity and very low oxygen can be expected to have prevented marine borers from living in the area and destroying wooden objects.

The relatively narrow center of the sea, between the Crimean peninsula on the north and the Anatolian coast on the south, seems to segregate the water motions into two independent gyres (circular current motions), which can be identified by their salinity. The shore line of the Black Sea is relatively smooth, with few coastal features, islands, bays, or inlets; generally, the underwater slope is steep and the 150-meter contour closely approaches the coast.

The upper limit of the deep, toxic water generally ranges from a hundred to a hundred and fifty meters, but occasionally animals have been found at depths of as much as two hundred meters. Presumably this indicates variations throughout the sea caused by seasonal changes or interfacial waves moving along the boundary between the two layers.

The tidal range in the Black Sea reaches a maximum of only eight centimeters on spring tides, but seasonal changes in sea level may be as much as thirty centimeters. Salinity in the upper layers (except around river mouths) averages 17–18 parts per thousand; in the deep water, it is about 22.5 parts per thousand except near the Bosporus, where it is somewhat higher. Very little of the sea surface freezes, but when the winter is severe, ice sheets form along the northern and western coasts and large masses of ice break off and float free. At the hottest times of the year, the same waters can reach 28° C (82° F).

In the open parts of the Black Sea, with depths over two hundred meters, the water transparency is such that a diver can usually see about twenty meters, with a maximum of thirty meters. Generally, this decreases near the coast, as it does in other seas. Visibility near the bottom in deep water has not been reported, but it can be expected to be at least five meters, which will be adequate for salvage work.

Figure 7. **The Black Sea**
This chart shows the western half of the Black Sea and the Sea of Marmara. The reducing environment is cross-hatched to show the huge extent of sea bottom that may contain extremely well-preserved ship hulks because no borers can live there and no oxidation can take place.

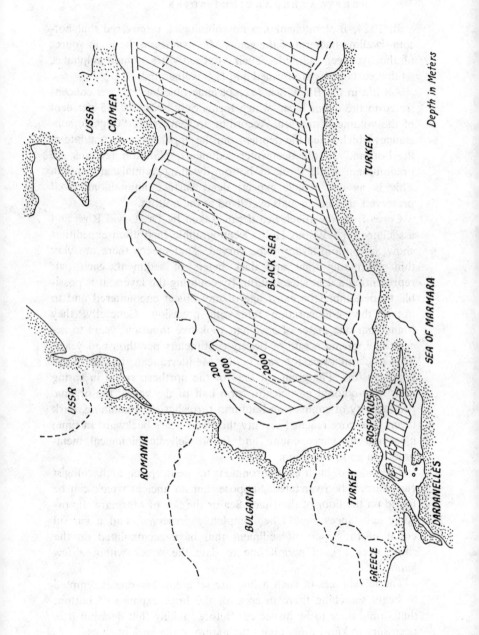

Depth in Meters

In 1924, B. Issatchenko, a microbiologist, discovered that bottom-dwelling bacteria of the genus *Microspira* are the main source of the hydrogen sulphide. Their vital activities reduce sulphates, so that carbonates are formed and H_2S is liberated.

All life in the Black Sea (except anaerobic bacteria) is concentrated in the upper layer, which forms only about 10–15 per cent of the volume of the sea. According to Zenkevich, "Organic substances which reach the depths from the upper layer accumulate at the bottom." In the deepwater sediments, plankton remains are predominant while those of bottom-dwelling animals are absent. This is as one would expect; dead surface animals are well preserved, and no animals ever lived at the bottom.

Cores from the Black Sea depths taken by Dr. David Ross and associates on a Woods Hole Oceanographic Institution expedition show the bottom strata to be varved. That means there are very thin alternating light and dark layers of sediment, each pair representing a year's deposition. By counting the layers, it is possible to determine the exact age of any object encountered and to obtain the sedimentation rate with precision. Generally, they found that one meter of sediment took five thousand years to accumulate, giving a rate of twenty centimeters per thousand years. This is about twice the rate in the Mediterranean, but there are good reasons. The great silt load of the northern rivers in spring adds light-colored particles to form half of the varve; the organic productivity of summer and autumn furnishes the remaining, dark layer. One core reached seventy thousand years backward in time, measured by varve count, and found delicate biological membranes in good condition.

The value of such an environment to the deep-sea archaeologist can scarcely be overstated. Suppose that an ancient wreck can be found on the floor of the Black Sea or the Sea of Marmara. Its organic substances should be completely preserved, and a careful count of the layers of sediment that have accumulated on the ship's deck should permit one to date the wreck within a few years.

The advantages of such a find are so great that one is tempted to begin searching there in spite of the huge expanse of bottom that would have to be inspected. Before making that decision it is necessary to know more about the nature of the ancient ships.

CHAPTER III

Warships

The searcher for old lost ships must know something about his quarry. Certainly the size, shape, and construction are useful pieces of information. Then it is helpful to know what sort of sea-resistant artifacts each class of ship carried and whether something valuable can be learned from retrieving those objects or from studying details of the ship construction methods. Finally it is important to know where the ships voyaged, so that sunken ones can be sought in areas of high probability.

This chapter will describe ancient warships, the way they were fought, and the city-states they served. As the ancient Egyptians said, "To speak of the dead is to make them live again."

The earliest known picture of seagoing warships was carefully carved on the tomb of a Pharaoh named Sahure in 2450 B.C.— two hundred years after Pharaoh Sneferu's forty ships brought cedars from Lebanon in the first recorded sea trade. The tomb drawing showed a fleet of troop transports carrying the Pharaoh's soldiers to some port in Asia. The ships look to be over thirty meters long, propelled by oars as well as sails. Obviously, they were the product of long years of development.

During the second millennium B.C., the people of the Aegean showed their strength at sea. The Minoans of Crete built a very high level of civilization, with cities and palaces that show no signs of defensive works. One explanation is that they relied on the same kind of "wooden walls" the oracle recommended to the Greeks during the Persian war a thousand years later. These wooden walls were fighting ships, ready to defend the island against all intruders. Thucydides wrote that "Minos is the first to whom tradition ascribes the possession of a Navy." According to Lionel Casson, "Their bold programs of overseas exploration and colonization, their far flung trade and their unwalled cities presupposes the existence of a great fleet." About 1500 B.C., the Minoan culture seems to have suddenly disintegrated. One hypothesis is that the great sea wave from the explosion of the volcano at Santorin wiped out the defending warships on the beaches and in the harbors along the northern coast. At any rate, by 1450 B.C. the fleet that had maintained order was gone and the chaos of sea raiders prevailed.

The Mycenaean Greeks then moved across the narrow channel from the Peleponnesus in strength and took over Crete, its colonies, and its commerce. Presumably they used warships, or at least troop transports, and readily subdued the Minoans, who were unprepared for land war. Mycenaean sea power rose quickly but faded in a few hundred years, leaving little trace. We do not know what their ships looked like; the record of those ships, if it exists, is on the sea floor.

As the Mycenaean grip on the seas began to slip, the rovers and pirates of Lycia (in southwestern Asia Minor) and the nearby isles—presumably Cyprus, Rhodes, and the Cyclades—banded together and formed raiding parties that swept the shores of the eastern Mediterranean. These rovers were contemporaries with the ones who became known as the "Sea Peoples," whose great, final sea battle with Ramses III, in 1194 B.C., is recorded in considerable detail on a famous relief at Medinet Habu, in the Nile delta. Ramses won decisively, apparently by some ruse, and now the Mediterranean stage was set for the Phoenicians.

One thinks of the Phoenicians as explorers and traders, which they certainly were, but they also seem to have been largely responsible for many early developments in fighting ships. In order to maintain their famous coastal cities (Sidon, Tyre,

Byblos) against raiders, as well as protect their merchantmen, the Phoenicians must have had a considerable navy. Certainly, they ventured to distant, unfriendly shores and dominated the eastern Mediterranean from 1100 to 800 B.C., although few details of their ships of that period are known. Later, in the fifth century, they minted coins showing fighting ships that were equivalent to those of the Greeks.

The first Greek ships of which we have a reasonably clear picture are the ones described by the poet Homer in the eighth century B.C. He told of the galleys of the Trojan War, in the Bronze Age, several hundred years earlier. The ships he described seem to have been a combination of those traditionally associated with Jason's Argonauts and the ships Homer saw about him. They were penteconters, long and slender, swift and black, painted with pitch except for the bow eyes. Such ships would have been about twenty meters long, low in the water and undecked. They were similar to, but probably less graceful than, the Viking ships of two thousand years later. They were built either for trading or raiding, as suited the captain's fancy. Such ships must have been light and strong, to permit frequent beachings and occasional portage. The rowing crew was fifty men, half on each side, one oar per man, and one steering oar on each side of the stern. There were also a mast and sail that could readily be stepped and rigged if there were a following wind. The crew would haul in on the forestays, raising the mast into its slot and tightening the backstay. Then they would hoist the single cross yard. The sail was square, probably of linen patches sewn checkerboard fashion between strengthening leather thongs, and supported from the yard, against which it was furled. The sail was raised and lowered by a series of lines called brails that looped around the foot, or bottom of the sail, so that it could be shortened by gathering it upward to the wooden yard, somewhat like a venetian blind.

Because the wind was contrary much of the time, the ship was often rowed. One such ship became known as the "hundred-handed giant of the Aegean"—a very apt description of fifty men rowing—not at all the mythical monster portrayed by some romantic artists. The ship would have been about wide enough to allow two men to sleep end to end on each rowing bench. With such accommodations, it is no wonder they preferred to go ashore every night to sleep on some soft beach where they could forage for food and build fires. Warships were not intended for good living even though the men that crewed them were sea rovers and adventurers used to rough conditions. Provisions, water in goatskin bags, and weapons were stowed under the benches. It must have been a hard life.

The oars were about four meters long and were levered against thole pins (vertical wooden pins that serve as lever points for the oars), being secured there by leather straps so that when the men dropped them to fight or to handle the sail the oars would not slide off and drift away. The steering oars, operated from the short, raised afterdeck, were also partly supported by leather thongs. Perhaps there was a sternpost, against which the steersman could brace himself. Because these ships were so low in the water, there may also have been a low rail along the sides to which some kind of a temporary screen of cloth or leather could be rigged—much as the Norsemen used shields two thousand years later to keep out the wind, the blown spray, and small waves.

Certainly the idea that a shipload of adventurers could circumnavigate the Black Sea as Jason and his fellow rovers did and bring back stories of hitherto unknown lands was pretty exciting. It must have seemed to their fellow Greeks as far out as a moon shot seems to us now, and a golden fleece is more romantic than a chip of moon rock. Tales of winged men (Babylonian statues), moving rocks (icebergs), and a witch princess (Medea) must have made the stay-at-homes tingle with vicarious delight. Eventually the tales became legend, but in the meantime the stories encouraged the development of better ships for adventuring.

Most warships, from earliest times until after the battle of Lepanto, in 1571, were galleys. They were driven by men's muscles, pulling on oars. Although most fighting ships of early times carried masts and sails for long passages at sea, sails were not dependable enough for fighting. Men were much better-disciplined than the wind.

Most of the naval engagements of the ancient world were probably fought within a mile or so of shore. This is because the ships were essentially land-based fighting tools. They were manned by soldiers and commanded by generals. In fights between ships, ordinary swords, missiles, and spears were used and the tactics were like those on land. The soldiers slept and ate on shore, drawing the ship up on a sandy beach every night, stern first, ready to shove off in a hurry to do battle. On long cruises, headed for some distant rendezvous with an enemy fleet, they tended to follow the shore lines and stay within sight of land rather than strike off across the sea. When they sailed, they could only run before the wind or with it on the beam, because of the flat-bottomed hull and square sail.

Doubtless, there were numerous times when these early warships had to cross wide passages out of sight of land—either rowing or under sail—and this they did only when necessary and always with trepidation. When King Nestor and his men returned to Greece from the Trojan War, in about 1200 B.C., he directly crossed the Aegean from Lesbos to Euboea, a distance of a hundred and ten miles, instead of the customary flitting from island to island for nightly camp-outs. At three knots, even on a somewhat zigzag course, this risky voyage took less than two days, but the expedition members were so pleased to reach the new shore safely they made a great sacrifice to Zeus. This episode unwittingly reveals quite a bit about the dangers to warships at sea in the Bronze Age. Since Nestor's courage is undoubted, there must have been a very bad record of ship losses, perhaps caused by the sudden violent winds and poor stability, to have made him so concerned. Possibly he wasn't certain about which direction to take, or he thought the sky would be cloudy and obscure the stars so he could not navigate, or he thought his boats had too little freeboard to survive a storm. Clearly, Nestor and his associates thought their open penteconters (which probably were loaded with booty and souvenirs) had a good chance of sinking as they crossed the deep water headed for home. Perhaps some did.

There are certain difficulties in training a large crew of men to row a ship. Anyone who has watched naval cadets rowing whale-boats, or crewmen from a large passenger liner practice with life-boats in a quiet harbor, has an inkling of the problem. Those are small craft with six to twelve rowers. Until the crew has had considerable practice, there is a great likelihood of "catching a crab" (the oar not digging deeply enough into the water and suddenly skittering along the surface when the power stroke is carelessly applied) or getting out of synchronization and tangling oars. In larger ships, with hundreds of rowers, it would be difficult to keep all the rowers in good health and a high state of training; there must have been many "crabs," bumped oars, and other foul-ups. Certainly a lot of practice was required to co-ordinate the actions of hundreds of men so that they rowed effectively in unison. The rowers had to learn to start and stop quickly, and to turn the ship in its own length by packing down on one side and pulling ahead on the other. But, in warships, they rowed as though their lives depended on it. Which they did.

War upon the sea in the early days, once it had developed beyond the stage of looting and taking slaves from coastal cities, had as its ultimate objective the control of sea-borne commerce. Piracy was the first step, but control of the trade routes and the establishment of colonies by a formal military machine were vital to expansion. The sea was the most convenient highway of the irregularly shore-lined Mediterranean, and the destruction of the ships of a city-state could cut off its food supplies and its colonies. The need for greater speed and power in sea battles led to the development of several new rowing schemes: several men on each oar, oars of different lengths on one slanted bench, and a second tier of oars mounted on the fighting deck above. The latter type of ship, the bireme, improved the speed without increasing the length or width.

Sometime in the ninth century B.C., the ram was invented. This led almost immediately to the development of the *triere,* or trireme as it is popularly known.

The trireme was a three-banked warship made specifically for fighting with the ram. It was a fast ship because it was slender and yet carried many more rowers than previous ships. This was made possible by the use of an outrigger beam to hold tholepins a bit above and outboard of the upper deck level. This arrangement permitted an entire new bank of rowers to be added without requiring longer oars or widening the hull. With this outrigger beam serving as an oar fulcrum, the oars of the upper rowers could reach out over the two banks of oars below. Now, using a one-man one-oar scheme, it was possible to add thirty-one men on each side (top row only—there were twenty-seven men in each of the other rows) and give the ship an additional ten horsepower of driving force. All oars were the same length, and the men were arranged in rows on half levels so that each bank of oars was at its most effective height. It was also necessary to position the oars so the individual rowers were not exactly one above the other. They were staggered a little so that each man (and each oar) had maximum space. One has to visualize the oar positions and motions in three dimensions for the diagrams to make sense. An additional advantage of increasing the number of rowers in the same length of ship was that this design also increased the number of fighters that could be quickly brought to bear on the enemy. The outrigger beam also squared up the deck shape with a sort of fence that held protective shields.

One limitation on going further with the idea of more oars upward and outward was ship stability—the extra weight high above the slim hull would have made it top-heavy. If there were a rush of armed men to one side to engage the enemy, such a ship would heel sharply and perhaps capsize.

Greek oared ships were carefully constructed and were much admired for their craftsmanship. The wood used for hull planking was mainly oak and poplar, often as much as eight centimeters (three inches) thick, carvel-fitted. This means the planks were joined edge to edge and held there by the mortise-and-tenon system of rectangular cavities with fitted pegs. The planks were also nailed to reinforcing ribs so the structure was secured together in two ways and would not fly apart on ramming or flex and leak after beaching. To make sure that the planks held together, it was customary to tie them together before a battle with several sets of girding cables which went completely around the ship. Before these came into use, many a ramming must have sunk the rammer as well as the intended victim.

The development of the ram reached its peak when the Athenians decided to put emphasis on a ship that would depend mainly on skillful ship handling. The ship itself, instead of the soldiers aboard, became the weapon. If it could be maneuvered to ram and sink an enemy ship, this would save much of the trouble of hand-to-hand fighting and war would be less personal.

There was real significance in the shift of strategy from trying to kill the enemy's men to that of trying to kill his ships. This had much the same kind of effect on naval warfare that the first cannon had much later. No one could ignore the new threat, and all navies began to build triremes.

Triremes were built ruggedly—able to ram or to survive ramming and, after repair, to fight another day. On many occasions, triremes were holed and capsized but remained afloat. The next day, they were towed ashore to be repaired and used again.

A good deal is known about the Greek trireme because, as the leading kind of warship for several hundred years, it was repeatedly described by historians, painted on vases, and sculptured in bas-reliefs. Unfortunately, these pictures are invariably a side view of the bow or stern of the ship and no complete representation has survived. As a result, no one knows exactly how the men were arranged or what a complete trireme looked like. The artists found that if all men and oars were shown there was too much detail, so it was customary to draw many of the oars but only a few men—and those greatly oversized.

We know what the three banks of rowers were named: thranites had the uppermost and most tiring position, zygites were between decks, and thalamites were in the lowest position (with their oars just above the water). We also know the size of Athenian triremes, because the foundations of the boathouses and launchways are still in existence. Visitors to Piraeus today can peer in basement windows on the harbor drive and see remnants of the slipways that once held these ships. Based on their size and configuration, the triremes that used them must have had flat bottoms and could not have been longer than forty meters or wider than seven. The records of the shipyard that built them, carved on stone tablets, were found lining a Piraeus storm sewer a few years ago. They list the exact amount of equipment issued to the ships: size and quantity of oars, anchors, sails, and line.

Although there must have been many varieties and sizes of triremes, most authorities agree that one set of dimensions and number of rowers predominated. The standard trireme of 500 B.C. was about thirty-five meters long, three and a half meters in the beam (five, including the outriggers) with a loaded draft of one meter and about 1.2 meters of freeboard. This meant these ships were very long and slender (fineness of 10:1), which is necessary for speed. In fact, they must have been much like an oversize racing shell, since they were light enough to be launched and dragged ashore by their crews.

The lowest oars were only about half a meter above the water line, so the hole where they penetrated the hull was sealed by a leather bag which could be bound to the oar to keep the water out. These ships had 170 rowers, each pulling an oar about 4.2 meters long. This arrangement, which permitted the use of short, standard-length oars, made the trireme a convenient ship to operate. The idea of standardized oar length for large numbers of ships suggests that somewhere there must have been a substantial production line turning out matched, interchangeable oars.

Each man was responsible for his own equipment: sword, shield, oar, and seat cushion. Sun awnings and spray shields were part of the ship's equipment, intended to keep the men as comfortable as possible.

Nearly every night, the ships were drawn up on some beach and drain plugs pulled to release the bilge water and keep the bottom planks from becoming soggy and rotten. Because the ships were light and slim, there was no way for the men to remain aboard; besides, very small amounts of stores and water were carried. This also meant that when away from their regular bases the crews had to forage for food and find entertainment; presumably, this often meant seizure and rape.

Although triremes were meant to be rowed in battle, each ship had a mast and sail that were used when there was a considerable distance to go and a wind on the stern quarter. If a battle was expected, the bulky mast and sail were left on shore. In fact, it was so much the custom for early warships to leave the sails and masts ashore, that carrying them into battle, even though they were stowed below, was regarded as a sign of cowardice, since it implied the intention to leave the battle early. Mark Antony's decision to take sails along into the great naval battle at Actium, in which he and Cleopatra VII were defeated by Octavian, is said to have demoralized his forces and contributed to his losing that battle.

Table 3. **Examples of Warship Losses in Battles and Storms**

Year B.C.	Combatants Winner	Loser	Location	Number of Ships Involved	Number of Ships Lost
535	Phoceans	Carthaginians and Etruscans	Corsica	180	100
480	Greeks	Persians	Salamis	1300	200
419	Syracuse	Athens	Harbor of Syracuse		350
333	Alexander	Tyre	Tyre Harbor	260	45
322	Macedonia	Athens	Amorgos (Sporades)	400	
306	Greeks	Egypt	Salamis, Cyprus		80
260	Rome	Carthage	Mylae	250	50
256	Rome	Carthage	Ecnomus	680	54
255	Rome	Carthage	Cape Hermaeum (storm)	620	284
255	Rome	Carthage	Camorina, Sicily		250
249	Rome	Carthage	Battle at Carthage and storm at Camorina	2 fleets	80
241	Rome	Carthage	Aegates Islands, Sicily	200	50
230	Rome	Illian pirates	Turkish straits	200	90
42	Agrippa	Sextus	Naulochus, Sicily	600	60
31	Antony and Cleopatra	Augustus	Actium, Gulf of Corinth	900	100

The circumstances of life in the trireme fleet were not at all like most people imagine. First of all, the rowers of ancient Greece were all free men—never slaves—and no whips were used. Stroke beat was kept by a flutist, probably because the high-frequency tootling was easy to hear above the rumble and splash of the oars. Rowers who were not soldiers were well paid, with extra pay for the men who pulled the uppermost, thranite oars, where the work was hardest and the danger greatest.

Triremes were not good sea boats; in fact, they were unusable in heavy weather and a great many more were lost in storms than in battle. They were so susceptible to loss in bad weather that they rarely operated in the winter months.

Historians have noted that for one reason or another pairs of galleys were sometimes lashed together and a single sail was hoisted. On some occasions, this may have been a ruse to make the enemy think he had half as many ships to deal with. However, it seems possible this was intended to improve stability, since each hull would prevent the other from rolling over. In time, this technique may have evolved into the catamaran warships that Professor Casson has postulated.

Another action that was taken to prevent these long ships from capsizing was to add ballast. Ballast may not always have been used on fighting triremes, but it was certainly used on troop transports and heavier galleys that were not intended to be drawn up on the beach. The ballast was usually in the form of sand or gravel carried in boxes in the bilges that could be removed separately to lighten the ship. Wet-sand ballast was used to keep wine jugs safe and cool as well as improve the ship's stability.

This is significant to the archaeologist. Unballasted wooden ships built for maneuvering and ramming would be "sunk" only in the sense they would fill with water and become unusable. Probably, the hulk would remain awash until it drifted ashore, was towed away, or became waterlogged and sank. But with ballast aboard, in addition to the weight of provisions in jugs, the ship fittings, the arms and armor, missiles for catapults, and souvenirs or booty from the enemy, there was a good chance a warship would go to the bottom immediately, taking these fascinating artifacts with it.

In the fourth century B.C., an arms race began when the city of Syracuse developed *tetreres* ("four-rowed" ships) to beat the Athenian *trieres* (or triremes). Although the changes in ship design came slowly at first, soon every navy in the ancient world was involved in building "fives," "eights," "tens," "thirteens," and so on up to a "forty." It is a marvelously intricate story of shifting naval power and how it was applied through great fleets of rowed ships. Ship weight, power, and stability increased at the expense of speed and convenience. Ramming became less important and instead battles were fought with catapults that flung rocks and arrows. Once again, ships grappled with each other and the rowers engaged in hand-to-hand fighting. Ptolemy II of Egypt eventually built the most powerful fleet in ancient times, which included four "thirteens," fourteen "elevens," thirty "nines," thirty-seven "sevens," and seven "fives." Unfortunately, we do not know what those numbers signify, because the exact meaning of the ending "eres," or "rowed," is lost. Presumably it is some combination of the number of tiers of oars and men on an oar.

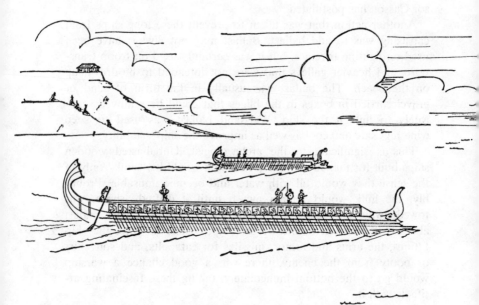

Figure 8. **Warships of the Fourth Century B.C.**

Triremes are shown moving into position for a ram attack on similar vessels of an enemy fleet. Triremes were long, slender ships, lightly built for use in coastal waters. The standard rowing crew of 170 men could propel these "manned torpedoes" at a maximum speed of about seven knots. Although they were not good sea boats, they were sailed between battle sites (often with heavy losses in storms); the sails and masts were left ashore when an engagement was expected.

Eventually the race subsided. After the battle of Actium, in 31 B.C., Rome ruled the Mediterranean and once again used triremes in its home fleet. In the course of the various struggles for power, especially that between Rome and Carthage, thousands of these ships were sunk. An estimate is that five thousand warships went down in deep water in ancient times. If one can be found, many of the above questions can probably be answered.

There is always the possibility of finding looted art objects and treasures on sunken warships or raiders. The Antikythera wreck previously mentioned seems to have been a cargo of Greek treasures looted by the Romans. The ship carrying this load of bronze and marble statues may have been running before the wind at night en route to Rome when it smashed into the rocky isle and sank. Very possibly other well-known finds, such as the Mahdia wreck and the Artemision statue wreck, were loot on the way to the captor's homeland.

The great imported stones and statues of Rome, including the obelisk in Vatican Square, were largely loot and could very well have sunk while at sea. It is evident that many such cargoes went down simply because there was so much traffic in stolen art objects. Nearly every conqueror brought back some major pieces to symbolize his triumph and to show examples of the culture of the conquered people. Probably the Achaeans carried home valuable pieces from Troy as Alexander did later from Tyre.

The likelihood of shipwrecks at such times was greater than usual. The winners may have seized the loot and skipped quickly before new forces could be brought against them—possibly leaving with war-damaged ships and tired and wounded men in the crews, without waiting for the most favorable weather. Or even if there was no need for haste, the ships may have been overloaded and manned by inexperienced and overconfident men. Or perhaps captured ships, whose seagoing qualities and characteristics were not well known, were used by the victors and were more easily lost.

The wrecks containing ancient artifacts need not have sunk in ancient times, for the lootings and losses have continued up to the present. Napoleon's troops found the Rosetta stone near Alexandria and removed it to France. Later, it was moved again to

England. Belzoni, the Italian strong man turned archaeologist, removed a colossal bust of Ramses II from Thebes and shipped it to the British Museum. A later shipment by Colonel Vyse, in about 1839, containing Egyptian tomb treasures including a royal sarcophagus, was lost at sea. (The British Museum, characteristically, is still keeping a place waiting in the Department of Egyptain Antiquities in case the sarcophagus ever turns up.) The Vénus de Milo was rescued from the sea, as was the bronze boy of Elba.

The Elgin marbles, part of the Parthenon frieze (regarded by most Greeks as loot and by the British as having been saved from a worse fate), were carefully crated and loaded on the *Mentor* in September 1802 and shipped to London. However, the ship had barely rounded legendary Cape Malea when it encountered a northwest gale and put into San Nikolo Bay on the isle of Kythera. There the *Mentor* dragged anchor and struck a rock, to sink in sixty feet of water. The famous marbles were salvaged but lay on the beach for a year until Lord Nelson sent another ship to take them the rest of the way to England. As Peter Throckmorton puts it, "Elgin had been only an English millionaire with a passion for antiquity who had done his looting at the end of the 1500 years of removal of Greek antiquities. Imagination boggles at what kind of material a Roman emperor like Hadrian or Nero might have been able to collect in a big ship."

Probably, looting, like virtue, reaps its own reward and the chances of a shipload of loot and looters being lost is somewhat greater than that of an ordinary merchantman or warship. Perhaps they deserved to sink, but their cargo would have been the richest kind—the cream of a civilization being carried away.

CHAPTER IV

Traders Under Sail

Less is known about the merchant ships of the ancient world than about the warships, although there were a great many more of them. They were the slow, solid workhorses of the sea; "round ships," they were called, to distinguish them from the slender fighting craft, which were the "long ships." The fate of nations hung on how well each kind of ship did its job, but the glamorous warships were the better recorded. Information on the merchant ships that carried the trade goods cheaply and slowly from port to port is very sketchy. The appearance of seagoing merchant ships in the sixth century B.C. is known because one unusually fine Greek black-figured bowl was carefully illustrated with two scenes of a pirate ship chasing and preparing to board a merchantman. In the first scene, the unsuspecting trading ship rides high in the water with the sail on its single mast mostly reefed. Beamy and slow compared to the sleek and menacing pirate galley, it is an easy prize, idling along with a single crewman manning the steering oars. The large, rectangular opening into the cargo hold takes up most of the deck space, and its high rim rises above the deck level to keep waves sloshing over the deck from reaching the cargo below. The sides of the cargo hatch show a pattern that seems to be lashings that hold down a covering tarpaulin. Aft of the helmsman, on the upcurved sternpost, there is the customary short ladder to be used by men to get off and on a beached or anchored ship. Another ladder-like structure, which runs the length of the ship, was probably used as a gangplank for carrying cargo from ship to shore.

In the second scene, the trader's crew has become aware they are an intended victim; the sail is down, filled with wind, pulling. But the merchantman cannot keep ahead of a pirate craft using both sails and oars. Probably the rest of the trader's crew are below, praying and getting weapons ready. Their life expectancy is short, or at least unhappy, because the pirates will likely make slaves of any who survive the takeover.

The accompanying sketch of an ancient merchantman is based on the old Greek drawing on the curved bowl. Because changes in ship design have traditionally come slowly, this simple hull and sail design remained in use for many centuries. Although no good drawings of the trading ships used for the next five centuries have survived, in the first century A.D. similar vessels are portrayed by Roman artists in paintings on house walls, mosaics at Pompeii, and bas-reliefs in stone. They are still beamy and round, steered with a pair of oars, and have a single, large mainsail supplemented with a smaller sail farther forward. Their afterdeck was a little higher, the over-all size was often larger, but the appearance and sail-handling methods were about the same.

No doubt, a sailor of 500 B.C. could have stepped aboard a ship built six hundred years later and unhesitatingly sailed it to its next port. He would check out the rigging, noting that the mainsail hung from a yard made of a pair of saplings whose butts were lashed together. The top of the sail would be securely bound to the yard with twine made of esparto grass, and its foot on each side would be bound to lines (the mainsheets) that came back to be secured to chocks within the helmsman's reach. By adjusting the length of the lines, hauling in the lee sheet, and slackening the windward one, a lone sailor could set the sail on a small ship. As the ship came to anchor or if a storm threatened, the mariners aboard would shorten sail, raising it by means of brail lines. The free end of these lines were secured to a transverse bar, also convenient to the steersman; the other end went up over the top of the yard, loosely down in front of the sail, and up behind the sail to be secured to the yard. By shortening these brail lines, the sail could be crumpled upward against the yard.

Steering by means of a pair of nearly vertical steering oars, one on each side of the stern, was the standard method throughout ancient times. These oars were supported in pairs of sockets by

Figure 9. **Merchant Ship, Sixth Century B.C.**
For at least a thousand years, small merchant ships must have looked much like the one portrayed here. Because they were short and broad, perhaps twenty meters long and six in the beam, they were known as "round ships," in contrast to the long, sleek warships. A ship of this size would carry about one hundred tons of cargo or twenty-five hundred amphorae and average about 4.5 knots running before favorable winds.

leather thongs so that they need only be rotated about their own axes to exert a rudder-like effect. At a convenient height, a short "tiller" bar projected from each oar at right angles so that the helmsman could easily twist the oar in its socket. To steer left (to port), he would push the tiller bar in his right hand ahead and pull back on the one in his left (the bars were always moved in opposite directions to keep the oar blades parallel). This gave a lot of rudder surface and was probably quite convenient. Moreover, it was a good thing to have a second rudder so the ship was not out of control if one oar snapped or the guides holding it in place gave way.

In order to ease the forces acting on the rudder, many early sailing ships carried a small sail forward on a steep bowsprit. This spritsail, or *artemon,* was used to keep the ship from yawing—sliding sidewise and forward down the face of an overtaking wave into a dangerous position. Since these ships sailed well only when running before the wind, the pull of the *artemon* kept the bow ahead of the ship. Probably it was the only sail used during storms, since it would keep the vessel from getting sidewise to the wind and waves and being overwhelmed by a breaking wave. In any case, it made the helmsman's job an easier one.

Another common feature was the boarding ladder, which shows in many of the old drawings of both war and merchant ships. These ladders enabled the men to climb aboard when the ship was on the beach or in the shallows close to it. It was carried at the stern (which is logical, since ships beached their rounded after ends first) and secured at its midpoint to the upswept sternpost. If a ladder was properly balanced, it could easily be swung down, used, and pushed up out of the way again.

Merchantmen also used long, ladder-like walkways for loading and unloading cargo. Significantly these are not shown on the ships after harbors with vertical stone piers came into use and a ship could tie up alongside and load or unload directly. But, in the days when cargoes were transferred across the beaches at the heads of small bays, the ship was securely moored just off the beach in very shallow water and the ladder was used as a bridge.

Like the warships, merchant vessels were beached for repair during the winter months. The bottoms were scraped to clean off the sea growth and then charred by holding blazing faggots against them to reduce marine-borer attack. The most seriously damaged planks were replaced. Teredos, the wooden hulls' worst enemy, took a heavy toll of ship bottoms that were not sheeted with lead beneath the water line. The lead was usually secured with copper tacks over a sealing fabric that was soaked in pitch or tar. If water became trapped between the lead sheeting and the planking, the wood would rot where it could not be seen, weakening the hull and sometimes causing it to break up in a storm. The results could be as bad as if borers had been there.

Many ancient ships were coated with tar and pitch and painted with colored wax to seal small holes and protect the wood against deterioration. Although the hulls were usually black from the tar, they often had bright-colored eyes and sternposts; red, violet, and gold seem to have been favored for superstructure decoration. Sails of linen or leather were sometimes assembled from multicolored patches or painted with symbols.

A bas-relief on an Egyptian tomb depicts in considerable detail Queen Hatshepsut's famous expedition to Punt (somewhere south along the eastern coast of Africa) around 1500 B.C. Her ships were large and beautiful and they brought home a fascinating collection of products. They were propelled by both sails and oars; a single mast amidships held a pair of long yards, to which the sail was attached; bow and stern ended in huge carved lotus blossoms.

Egyptian ships had three distinctive characteristics. One was a second yard at the foot of the sail supported by many lines to the masthead. Their system was to furl the sail by lowering the upper yard—quite different from the brailing system just described that was used a thousand years later. The second special Egyptian feature was a tensioning hawser running fore and aft above the deck which literally tied the bow to the stern. Each end of the ship was held in a large loop of line. Then the connecting hawser was tightened by jamming a line of props under it and twisting a tourniquet-like device so that it acted to support the ends of the ship. In effect, the shipbuilders were trying to make a beam with no compression member at the top. The need for this structural change seems to have arisen when craft designed for the Nile

River were adapted for rough water; the simple keelless wooden hulls they used on inland waters would not hold together in a seaway where waves tended to flex the ship. The third characteristic of Egyptian ships was the double mast, much like a slender A-frame. This was necessary because without a keel there was not enough strength in the bottom planking to step an ordinary mast. So they put one leg of the double mast on each gunwale and divided the weight between the sides.

Much of the inscription that goes with the painted bas-reliefs on the temple walls tells of the cargo contained by Hatshepsut's ships: "The ruler of Punt came to the ships with tribute, and they were loaded with wonderful products from this land of the Gods. There were many kinds of wood, incense, pungent gums, monkeys, dogs, leopard skins, and people." What the Egyptians gave in return, how many ships made the voyage, how long they stayed, and even where Punt is (it may have been near Zanzibar) are not known.

The flaws in basic ship structure and design, plus the fact that all large timber had to be imported, were probably the reasons that Egyptians never became a really great seagoing power in the Mediterranean. However, they did voyage throughout the eastern Mediterranean as well as south along the African coast and left a faint trail for us to follow.

Proceeding farther back in time, to 2650 B.C., one comes to the first recorded trading voyage: the famous forty ships that brought cedar logs to Egypt from Lebanon for Pharaoh Sneferu. Obviously, there was well developed trade long before this time (forty shiploads could hardly have been an initial order), but the records of all the other voyages are lost.

Just when seagoing trade originated in the Mediterranean is not known, but there are many hints that for two or three thousand years before the earliest ship drawing, people were moving and carrying objects with them that they must have traded. In this haze of prehistory, one good sign of trade contacts between people is the finding of some unique natural substance that could only have come from an identifiable source elsewhere. Obsidian, or volcanic glass, is one such trade material that came into general use about eight thousand years ago, in the Stone Age. Obsidian

1. This lifelike bronze head of "The Philosopher" was recovered in 1900 by Greek sponge divers from the wreck of a ship that crashed into the cliffs of Antikythera in 82 B.C. (*Greek National Museum*)

2. "The Jockey Boy," a third-century-B.C. bronze found near Cape Artemision in 1927, is one of a number of great statues salvaged from a wreck that
was abandoned and lost before the excavation was completed. With modern
technology, it should be possible to find the site again. (*Greek National
Museum*)

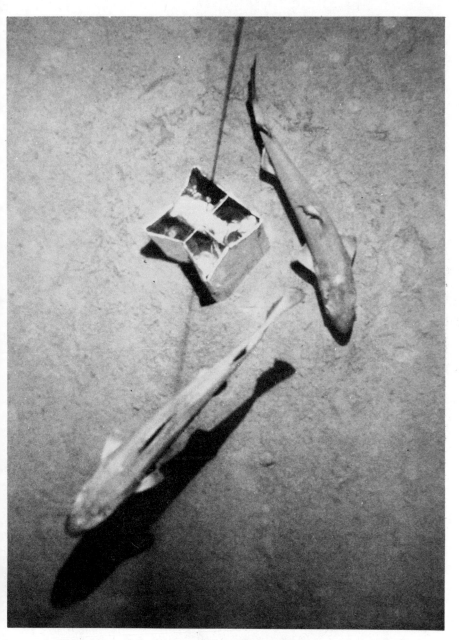

3. This picture of the bottom of the eastern Mediterranean was made by John Isaacs of the Scripps Institution of Oceanography at a depth of 880 meters (2700 feet). The muddy character of the sea floor, the clarity of the water, and the existence of large fish, indicating ample dissolved oxygen, are all important to the searcher for ancient ships. (*J. D. Isaacs, University of California*)

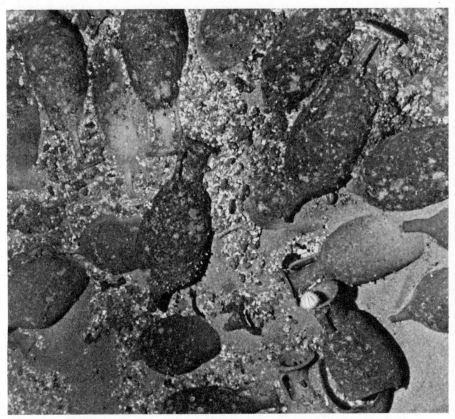

4. Amphorae on ancient wreck in the Strait of Gibraltar between Tangier and Trafalgar at a depth of about 400 meters (1250 feet). This photo was made from the oceanographic ship *Amalthée* during a study of a gas-pipeline route for S.E.G.A.N.S. (*George Orlotan*)

5. Many amphorae can be identified by their style as to place of origin and date of manufacture. Since every ship carried at least a few, they will be a great help in dating and identifying wrecks. M. J. Franjud of the Musée d'Adge prepared these examples. (*L'Aventure Sous-Marine*)

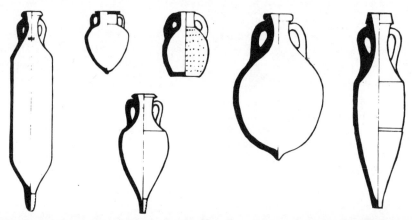

tools have been found in many early village sites around the Mediterranean although its source is only a few specific volcanoes, often hundreds of miles away on islands or across the sea.

By means of spectrographic techniques, J. E. Dixon and other scientists discovered that it is possible to detect certain trace elements in very small samples of this volcanic glass. Two elements, zirconium and barium, were found to be present with the greatest quantitative variation. This meant that if the investigators could establish the ratios of those two elements to each other at each major volcano, they could thenceforth identify the source of any piece of obsidian. Thus, an obsidian tool might bear an unmistakable chemical fingerprint that would give clear evidence of early trading voyages. Among neolithic temples of Malta, where no obsidian occurs naturally, tools were found that had been imported from Lipari and Pantelleria, a hundred and fifty miles away. The people who built these temples had themselves come by sea long before, possibly during the ice ages. The use of obsidian for tools declined with the coming of the metal ages, after 4000 B.C., but by tracking its movements in the time when it was essential to human progress, we can learn something of the origins of seagoing trade.

More is known about the likely routes the merchant ships followed than about the ships themselves. The reason is evident. The ports and harbors used were the ones that would be selected by any seafarer, then or now. Sailors want harbors sheltered by projecting headlands and islands offshore so that their ships are protected from wind and waves. The ancient mariners wanted places to stop at frequent intervals so that if the weather suddenly "made up," the ship could duck into a safe place and incidentally get fresh water, food, and firewood. They wanted places to trade for wine and girls, as has every other sailor since.

Facilities of all sorts began to develop in the sheltered bays along the routes where ships generally sailed. Shaped stone was used for breakwaters, piers, and buildings, and many of those foundations still survive. In some places, the tops of the breakwaters have been pounded down below present sea level by twenty-five centuries of wave action, but they can still be seen as dark-green shadows beneath the light-green sea. In other areas, change in relative sea level caused by tectonic movements of the coast has raised waterfront structures to improbable heights or plunged the surfaces of piers and the floors of buildings several meters below the present sea surface. Fragments of hundreds of such ancient coastal towns can be found along the Mediterranean coast line. Most are still inhabited and some have become large cities, but others have reverted to desert or sunk beneath the sea.

If one combines a general knowledge of the sorts of goods that were shipped and the cities that were major importers with information on the winds and the evidence of ancient port structures, one can get a good idea of the locations of the ancient trade routes.

Mostly the routes ran along coasts or hopped between islands at convenient points so that the tradesmen were rarely out of sight of land. They were also rarely out of the sight of pirates, who would lie in wait in the lee of deserted headlands hoping for a rich-looking prize that could be attacked.

Probably there were jumping-off ports where ships and their crews waited out bad weather, the sailors alternating between temples and wineshops, between praying and cursing. On the longer overseas voyages such as those from Cyprus to Egypt or Sicily to Alexandria, bad weather must have caused ships to accumulate at the last safe port until the harbor was jammed. The fleet might wait weeks for a favorable wind, and then all of a sudden one clear morning, sail off together, wagering on who would reach the next port first but gaining confidence from each other's presence. In pirate-ridden areas, traders often sailed in groups for mutual defense.

Sporadic trading by itinerant vessels must have begun long before the dawn of written history. But as the population grew and cities developed, a more systematic method of obtaining supplies from afar was needed. In the beginning, each state sent out trader-adventurers to dispose of its surplus products. They had to travel at least far enough to get to a place that had different products. The cities of the Black Sea coast sought outlets to the south; the Egyptians pushed north along the Levant coast and west to Malta; the Minoans reached Sicily and the Italian peninsula. Unfortunately, there is no record of these brave adventurers who put their lives at risk every time they landed on a new shore or headed out across the unknown sea with only a vague notion of where they might next touch land.

In time formal trading agreements were made between home ports and a series of distant outposts that required merchant vessels to follow a route and regularly call at certain ports as they sailed in each direction. So the trade routes developed, each one implying a stream of ships moving between ports in organized and routine commerce.

The Phoenicians were the world's leading traders at the time sea routes were pioneered and ship schedules first became systematic. No point was too distant for their trading ventures, and in a few hundred years they knew the Mediterranean well and passed beyond it into the Atlantic, spreading down the coast of Africa, north along the Spanish coast, outward to the Canaries and beyond.

Phoenician traders were remembered for their dark complexions and distinctive purple cloaks. They were Canaanites, whose homes were the ports of Byblos, Tyre, and Sidon, on the narrow Levantine coastal plain. Geography sent the Phoenicians to sea. The powerful neighbor states to the north and south prevented expansion in those directions; there were arid mountains behind, luckily covered with cedars, and the sea was before them. So they cut the cedar to build ships and went to sea. Traces still remain of their ancient harbors; the old breakwaters and moles can be seen beneath the clear waters, and old foundations dot the coast. Behind the cities, one can still see piles of murex shells, whose inhabitants furnished the dye for the purple cloaks of the old sea traders.

The trading led to the establishment of agents, outposts, and settlements, some of which eventually grew into great cities. Gades (Cadiz), on the Atlantic coast of Spain, was established in the twelfth century; Utica, not far from the eventual site of Carthage, was set up about 1100 B.C.; and Motya, at the western tip of Sicily, was founded in the eighth century. The Phoenician strategy was to control the narrow Straits of Sicily from the cities of Utica and Motya, on opposite shores, and to prevent competitors from using the Strait of Gibraltar by means of a blockade. Those who got beyond those passages and called ashore would find Phoenicians waiting at Gades to the north protecting the tin of Tarshish as well as the seagoing tin routes to Britain. Those who turned south came to Mogador (near Casablanca, Morocco), a city that tapped the lush resources of northwestern Africa.

In the eighth century B.C., the Phoenician successes attracted competition. At that time, the Greeks were not a unified people but a collection of city-states around the borders of the Aegean Sea. Rumors of Phoenician ventures in the west spread by sailors in waterfront bars encouraged a new program of expansion, and city-states set about building new and larger ships. Each one acted independently, and often there were violent clashes between them in the competition to set up distant trading posts.

Between 750 and 550 B.C., the Greeks founded some two hundred and fifty colony-cities most of which were seaport towns around the Mediterranean and Black seas and some of which have been continuously inhabited ever since. The city-state of Corinth founded Syracuse on Sicily; Miletus established Sinope and Trapezus on the Black Sea and Sybaris in the arch of the Italian boot; Megara set up Byzantium in the Turkish straits; and Sparta established Tarentum at the tip of the heel of Italy.

The new cities were used as trading points and distribution centers for the home countries' products: pottery, wine, textiles, metals, oil, grain—the essential commodities of the day. The oil and wine trade route that led from the eastern Aegean island of Chios down the Ionian coast to Samos, Rhodes, Cyprus, and then directly to Naucratis in Egypt was started then and used for a thousand years. The dozens of wrecks found by Peter Throck-

Figure 10. **Trade Routes**
The Phoenicians are believed to have developed the original Mediterranean trade routes that were followed by merchant vessels for thousands of years. The dashed lines indicate some of the most heavily traveled routes in the eighth to sixth centuries B.C. and the names of some of the principal ports.

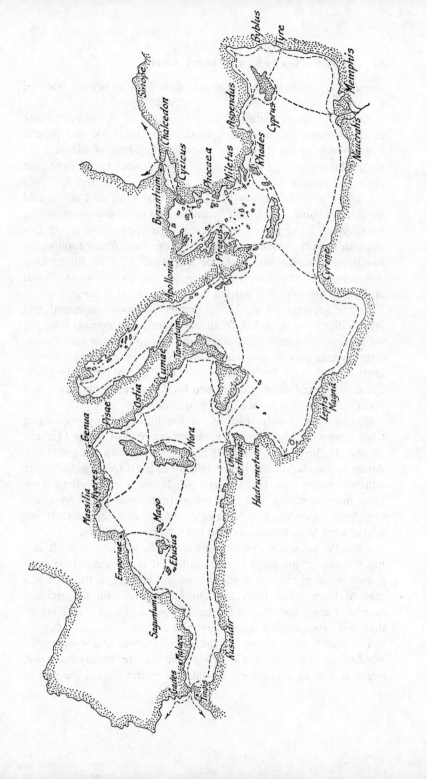

morton on shoals along that route attest to how heavily traveled
it was.

Another famous route led from Phocaea, on the eastern shore
of the Aegean, through the Cyclades Islands, down and around
Cape Malea to the tip of Italy, through the Strait of Messina, up
the Italian coast, and eventually to Hyeres, near the present port
city of Marseilles.

Corinth, astride the low hill between the Gulf of Corinth and
the Saronic Gulf, could send its sailors and products either east or
west. Along all of its sea trails, great quantities of the lovely Co-
rinthian pottery moved; samples of it have been found around the
Mediterranean. To the west, the ships sailed to its enterprising
new colony of Syracuse. The city grew rich, but we know almost
nothing of the ships that carried the trade goods that made it so.

In the seventh century, the commercial boom increased and
more cities were founded. With experience and competition, the
sea traders became a bit more daring; seafaring men chose more
direct routes across open waters. A flow of products also moved
northward through the Turkish straits past Byzantium to the Black
Sea cities. Trade steadily developed for the next few centuries, and
grain, oil, and wine moved in huge quantities.

By the fifth century, Piraeus, at the hub of many convergent
trade routes, had become the most important port in the Mediterranean. Its large and well-built harbor, along with the growth of
Attica in population and industrialization, led it to eclipse all other
marine centers. In the western Mediterranean, Carthage, the
most important city, had established trade monopolies in weapons, tools, precious metals, jewelry, ivory, and ceramics. It imported wine from Rhodes and oil from Acragas in Sicily.

After the colonizing period was over, the volume of trade and
the number of the ships in use continued to increase. Important
routes included the one from Piraeus to Syracuse, a trip that was
said to have taken from nine to eleven days on an ordinary
merchant ship, and the one from Piraeus to Egypt, via Rhodes,
that took seven to nine days to complete.

The fourth century saw the decline of Piraeus and a shift eastward of the major centers of trade. Antioch, on the Syrian coast,
began to rise in importance, as did Alexandria toward the end of

the century. Rhodes was flourishing as a great maritime nation and soon became a model trade city. To the west, Ostia, a port of Rome, was beginning trade with Gaul, Spain, North Africa, and all the ports of the eastern Mediterranean.

From the third century B.C. on, the Romans were in ascendancy. Corinth was burned, Carthage was sacked, and Syracuse was reduced. Tyre and Sidon slipped from importance; now Rome ruled the waves. Puteoli became the "hub of trade" for the Roman republic, and it dealt with the newer cities of Alexandria, Caesarea, and Leptis Magna as well as Rhodes and Delos. A grain fleet of large ships sailed regularly between Puteoli and Alexandria, driven down by the northwest winds in about nine days. The return trip from Alexandria back to Rome was a longer run with many stops; it took nineteen days if the weather was good, possibly months if it was bad.

There were many hazards along the Rome-Alexandria grain route, and many ships were lost. Even so, Professor Casson believes that the creation and maintenance of this fleet was Rome's single greatest maritime achievement. It was both a freight and a passenger service, and the vessels, like most other merchantmen, were owned, commanded, and crewed by Greeks and Phoenicians. The Romans were not good sailors; rather, they contributed a genius for organization and administration. For size of vessels and volume of cargo moved, this route had no equal for another fifteen hundred years.

The number of ships in use in ancient times that could have sunk along the trade routes is of great interest to the archaeologist. Fred Yallouris, a native of the island of Chios and student of classics, estimated how many ships had been in use in ancient times as follows: "The life-span of the merchant ship must have been around 40 years. The numbers we have suggest that in the fifth and fourth centuries B.C., well over 30,000 merchants ships of all sizes could have been built. Allowing for a lower building rate in the tenth to sixth centuries B.C., say 45,000, and an increase in the third to first centuries B.C., say 80,000, we arrive at an amazing 155,000 as the approximate number of merchant ships that sailed from 1000 B.C. to the beginning of the Christian era. If we were to extend our period of interest to include all the ships which sailed from the fourth millennium B.C. down to about 500 A.D., and also include warships, then that number could easily reach half a million."

Almost every port had some type of shipbuilding activity, but the larger ports, with greater merchant and naval fleets, dominated ship construction. We know that Tyre, Piraeus, Rhodes, Corinth, Alexandria, and Rome were great shipbuilding centers, but we do not know how many ships they produced. However, there are data on the docking capacity of some ports. Piraeus had, by 331 B.C., 372 docks in its three basins and could accommodate hundreds of ships, as could the harbors at Syracuse, Carthage, Rhodes, Alexandria, and the ports of Rome. The capacities of medium-sized ports such as Chios, Samos, Smyrna, Miletus, Antioch, Sidon, Tyre, Massilia, and Cyrene probably ranged from fifty to a hundred and fifty ships. The hundreds of smaller ports could probably harbor from twenty to fifty vessels.

There must have been close to four hundred ports in the Mediterranean by the end of the fourth century B.C. The average capacity of all these was probably around forty ships. Assuming that an average port was filled to about half capacity every night in the sailing season, we might reckon that from eight to ten thousand merchant ships could have been in use on the Mediterranean and the Black seas throughout the fifth and fourth centuries. The number could well have reached fifteen thousand at the height of Rome's commercial activities in the second and first centuries.

Another way of obtaining the flow of sea trade about the ancient world is to estimate the population of the various city-states and then to consider their requirements for trade goods from foreign lands.

Attica in the fifth century B.C. had a total free population of about 150,000 citizens, plus some twenty thousand aliens living in Athens and Piraeus and over a hundred thousand slaves. Athens itself housed perhaps a hundred thousand of the total, and twenty other cities had, on the average, fifty to sixty thousand people (including slaves and aliens). Then there were perhaps another twenty towns with a population of ten thousand each. By the fourth century, Syracuse (on Sicily) became the largest of the Greek cities, with a total population of over a hundred thousand.

Corinth had seventy thousand; there were hundreds with five thousand people. There were fifteen hundred Hellenic cities and towns all told. The population of all Greeks (cities, towns, and remote areas) must have been about three million persons in the fifth and fourth centuries B.C.

Using these population figures, we can roughly estimate how many ships may have been required to satisfy the import needs of the people of Greece in the fifth century B.C. If there were three million people, of whom one third lived partly off grains coming from the shores of the Black Sea or Egypt, then the following calculation gives us a hint at the quantity of international trade.

A standard amphora of those times held about thirty-five liters, and a medium-sized ship would carry twenty-five hundred amphorae. Two liters of grain would produce about one of flour and be roughly equivalent to three large loaves of bread. Allowing three loaves of bread a week per person, this is two liters of grain per person, or about a hundred liters per year.

One third of the total population of three million people would then consume a hundred thousand liters a year of imported grain (assuming the remainder of the populace lived entirely off local products). This is three million amphorae of grain, or twelve hundred shiploads. If each ship made four voyages per season, there were three hundred fair-sized ships in the Greek grain trade alone. At least another three hundred ships were required to carry the other food commodities (wine, olive oil, nuts, pickled fish) on the longer trade runs in the Aegean, Black, and eastern Mediterranean seas.

Hard commodities such as metals, stone, timber, and fabricated goods also moved along the trade routes; some of these items fulfilled long-term bulk contracts but others were exchanged at any harbor for local products. A network of land traders met the ships and carried the products inland for resale. Some ships were simply floating workshops: tinkers making and selling tools, knives, utensils; shipfitters making metal parts for ships, replacing rotted planks, selling line and spars; armorers selling weapons and protective armor.

There were also local trading vessels, ferries, and fishing craft working out of and plying between the hundred-odd ports of the

Greek archipelago. If each port built one ship per year, this would be twenty thousand ships in two hundred years, considering only part of the eastern Mediterranean. This agrees moderately well with Yallouris' calculation of thirty thousand ships at sea in the two hundred years of the fifth and fourth centuries for the entire Mediterranean.

The above estimates of the number of ships and volume of shipping in ancient times are admittedly rough, but they seem reasonable and are probably close to the truth. At least they give the distant observer a feeling for maritime commerce in the ancient world.

Navigation must have been a serious problem for the early mariners. Although the development of navigational know-how cannot be traced precisely, we know that by the end of the fifth century B.C. most of the techniques that sailors would use for the next two thousand years were known. Of the later tools, only the magnetic compass was missing. Mainly, the early ships must have navigated by dead reckoning combined with the captain's memory.

Dead reckoning simply means that the skipper keeps track of the ship's course, its speed, and the elapsed time. From these data, he calculates how far the ship has gone and in which direction. For old sailing ships, which followed the wind and did not have a compass, a clock, or a good chart, the answer must have been, at best, a rough approximation. But perhaps because Mediterranean sailing distances are not great, the ancient mariners found their way fairly well. After years of apprenticeship, a sailor would learn the routes and how best to sail each leg of a voyage in each season. He would judge the ship's speed by tossing chips of wood overside and set its direction relative to the sun or stars if he could see them.

The knowledge of how and where to sail through the complex islands of the Aegean or across the Mediterranean to another country was largely kept in the captain's head. This special knowledge was his job security, and probably he did not want it written down so that someone else could replace him. On voyages of exploration, when new trading partners for valuable commodities were being located, the courses and distances were carefully guarded strategic secrets. At times, Phoenician vessels were followed by the ships of other countries eager to find where they traded for rare products. It is said that on more than one occasion Phoenician captains deliberately ran their ships through very dangerous waters and sometimes wrecked them in order to wreck the following ship or at least throw it off the track. Their country reimbursed them for the loss when they finally made it home.

By the fourth century B.C., a geographer named Scylax the Younger wrote a book (the Periplus), which gave the first published sailing directions for the Mediterranean. It contained the names of ports, rivers, and headlands, directions and distances from point to point, where to get water, and other useful information. Any charts of that time that may have existed were probably lost in the fires at the library of Alexandria in 47 B.C. and A.D. 640, or disintegrated over the ages.

Although there is virtually nothing in ancient literature that can tell us how many ships were lost at sea, there is no doubt that shipwrecks were a common phenomenon in antiquity. The Romans developed a code of maritime laws that eventually grew into a compendium called the Rhodian sea laws. It regarded pirates, fire, and wreck as the three normal maritime dangers, and had laws concerning all three. Three kinds of pirates were described: ". . . those who attack the merchantmen in open sea or lurk for them in harbors. Secondly there are the land-robbers, who cut a ship's cables or steal its anchors, or snap up a merchant or passenger or sailor who happens to go on land. Thirdly, there are the wreckers, and these do not merely plunder ships which have been driven ashore, but sometimes lure them to destruction by displaying false lights."

The danger of fire on board was always present. Although there is no way of ascertaining how many ships were lost in this way, it is evident from the strict laws regarding fires on board ship that loss of ship by fire was quite common.

Shipwreck was the usual way to lose a ship, however, and the sea laws discuss running aground, breaking up on the rocks, collision with other ships, seams opening up, and foundering in open water. A few excerpts from the sea laws will be of interest. No. 28: "If a ship is hindered in the loading by a merchant or

partner, and the time fixed for loading passes, and it happens the
the ship is lost by reason of piracy or fire or wreck, let him who
caused the hindrance make good the damage."

No. 26: "If a ship in sail runs against another ship which is lying
at anchor or has slackened sail, and it is day, all the damage shall
be charged to the captain and those who are on board. Moreover
let the cargo too come into contribution. If this happens at night,
let the man who slackened sail light a fire. If he has no fire, let
him shout. If he neglects to do this and a disaster takes place, he
has himself to thank for it, if the evidence goes to this. . . ."

No. 45: "If in the open sea a ship is overset or destroyed, let him
who brings anything from it safe to land receive instead of reward,
the fifth part of that which he saves."

As we have seen, a great many merchant ships crisscrossed the
seas in ancient times, often on voyages that turned out to be dangerous. Many were lost. Next, we will examine statistics that can
be used to estimate how many ships may be down in the protection of deep water.

CHAPTER V

Ships to the Bottom

As every shipowner and captain knows, there are an astonishing number of ways a ship can get into trouble at sea. Lloyd's of London, the great meeting place of ship insurers and brokers, discovers new ones nearly every week. The ships they insure these days are mainly made of steel, driven by engines and propellers, but not so long ago they were wooden sailing ships. Lloyd's men have kept good records of both kinds of ships and, in terms of loss statistics, there is not as much difference between them as one might think. Modern ships, often equipped with excellent navigation equipment, automatic fire extinguishers, and radar warning systems, still manage to run aground, catch fire, and collide. Some explode for unexplained reasons; others break up when the sea is relatively calm. This is mentioned to make the point that ship losses are a frequent occurrence today, in spite of all the technical advances that have been made in safety and navigation. In ancient times, the percentage of loss must have been very much higher.

We are concerned here with losses of wooden sailing ships, which make up about 95 per cent of all ships ever built. Their worst hazard was in running aground at night or being blown on shore by a storm. We will only briefly consider this type of wreck, because the main concern of this book is with ships that went down in deep water. Statistics for the eighteenth and nineteenth centuries indicate that approximately 40 per cent of all wooden sailing ships ended their careers by running onto reefs, rocks, or beaches made of rock, sand, or coral. This is a fantastic number of ships, perhaps as many as three hundred thousand per century for the world's oceans. However, at least another 10 per cent, and possibly as many as 20 per cent, of all wooden sailing ships sank well offshore, creating a target for the deepwater archaeologist.

The reader is reminded that although wood floats and many kinds of wooden vessels will remain afloat even though they are filled with water, sailing ships invariably carry ballast to help them stay upright in the water. This ballast is some heavy material placed low in the hull, just above the keel, to lower the center of gravity of the ship relative to the center of buoyancy and give it greater stability. Through most of history, rocks have been used for this purpose (generally these are stream-worn, rounded cobbles that have no sharp edges to gouge or chafe the planking from the inside), but sand, clay bricks, and old military iron have also been extensively used. The point is that this material is heavy enough to drag down a water-filled hull that might otherwise have stayed afloat.

Previously it was noted that triremes, which were both sailed and rowed, sometimes had removable ballast, and we cannot be sure whether they sank to the bottom or not, but virtually all merchant sailing ships were ballasted. Since the ballast was usually made up of many small rocks not cemented in place, it was possible for ballast to shift position if the ship rolled hard, readjusting itself downward toward the lee side. This, of course, prevented the ship from returning to an even keel and no doubt contributed to numerous sinkings. The famous Swedish warship *Wasa,* salvaged from the bottom of Stockholm Harbor in 1961, apparently rolled over because it was underballasted (presumably, the naval architect's plan was not followed carefully). Even so, the weight of ballast, cannon, and stores was enough to sink the ship once it filled with water. In searching for old shipwrecks, one looks for humps on the bottom, which will exist even if the wood has long since disappeared, caused by the indestructible ballast pile. Any pile of rocks on the muddy sea floor is almost certainly the ballast of a ship.

It is also worth remembering that most of the Mediterranean and Black seas is deep. This means that ships may spend most of their time over deep water. Sailing ships found security in being as far from shore as possible in a storm and would deliberately run to sea in a blow if no harbor was nearby.

Why did ships sink in deep water? Let me count the ways. Wooden sailing ships were subject to the following kinds of mishaps:

1. The ship can be overwhelmed by the conditions at sea. Winds at whole-gale force, with velocities of fifty knots or more, can, by brute force, blow a ship over. Even if all the sails have been taken in (or blown out) and the ship is running before the wind on bare poles, the rudder can fail or the helmsman make a mistake and the ship can broach (turn sidewise to wind and wave) and capsize. Or a ship may be low in the water because of leaks or overloading. With low freeboard, the lee rail easily goes under; then perhaps the cargo will shift or the deck will leak and the list will increase until the ship cannot right itself again. Or a ship blown hard before the wind, perhaps built with a sleek bow for speed, will drive into the back of a huge wave and be taken by the sea in one gulp. On other occasions, not necessarily in very high winds, a ship running on one tack will suddenly pass through a weather front into winds coming from exactly the opposite direction. Then the square sails will flatten back against the masts and the ship will be blown over backward in a matter of seconds. Open hatches or scuttles, now on the low side, let the sea pour in and the ship is gone.

This quick wind reversal can also be achieved by waterspouts (sea tornadoes), which are much more common than most landsmen realize. These are concentrated violent winds with a rotating vortex of small diameter that extends upward for hundreds of meters. Waterspouts may actually be attracted to ships, but, in any case, a slow-sailing ship would have a hard time avoiding a fast-moving spout. As one passes, the rapidly rotating winds shift from port to starboard and over goes the ship. Probably quite a few ships have been lost in this fashion.

2. Wooden ships are generally built of bent planks nailed to rib timbers or, in ancient times, mortised edgewise to each other carvel-style. It is quite possible for a nail to corrode through or a tenon to rot so the planks come free of each other and pull away from the rib. Instantly, there can be huge leaks, far beyond the capacity of hand pumps to stem. Since sailing ships were rarely compartmented with transverse bulkheads, as modern ships are, the hull could rapidly fill with water and sink.

A more serious variation of this mishap could arise if the whole ship structure were so weak that the ship flexed as waves passed beneath it. With a wave crest at the center and the bow and stern relatively unsupported (or vice versa) there is always minor bending of the ship's structure. But if the ship flexes too much it can come apart; the deck crumples or pulls in two, the ribs spread, the seams open, the mast falls, and its stays rip out the shear strakes. The ship can quickly become a mass of kindling wood.

3. Ships collide under many sets of circumstances. Usually, one thinks of collisions happening in restricted waters, but open-ocean collisions occur too. The ships may be running at night and neither helmsman sees the other in time to steer clear—especially if one is overtaken from the rear. Or two strong-willed captains each insist on the right of way (very common in sailboat races) or the inside track around a headland. Such circumstances might result in a collision or a sideswipe, either of which might be enough to crumple a few planks and let the sea in. All these cases of plank failure are aggravated if the wood has been weakened by marine borers or rot. The fact that modern ships, equipped with radar and well lighted, still collide hints at the ancient problems.

4. Some ships have been lost because they were poorly designed or not built exactly as designed. Shipbuilding may look easy, but the details of how each timber or plank is joined, as well as the choice of woods and fasteners, are very important. In an effort to make ships go faster, they are made slimmer—which also may mean they roll over easily. The position and height of the mast, the size of the sail, the weight and location of the ballast—all are important in how well a ship survives at sea. It is obvious that not all the little shipyards around the Mediterranean could have had

men who thoroughly understood the significance of these matters. They built small ships that looked about like the ones they saw. But small differences in the rake and position of the mast, the depth of the keel, the size or rigging of the sail, and the way the cargo is loaded, make a great deal of difference in the way a ship sails.

The same sort of reasoning can be applied to the men that sailed the ships. Some were good, careful, and lucky; others were the opposite. There is much to know about sailing a ship, and there were plenty of opportunities for a serious mistake as the wind changed abruptly, or strange shores appeared, or a menacing craft approached.

5. Wooden ships caught fire with remarkable ease. At night or below deck, oil lamps were used for light; it is easy to imagine that these could be spilled in such a way that blazing oil could run down the ribs and planking into the bilge or other areas where it would be hard to extinguish. Cooking fires could be an even more efficient cause of disaster. Glowing coals, usually restrained by cooking tiles and grating, would be thrown onto the deck by a lurch caused by a sudden large wave or by the ship coming about on the other tack. The dumping of red-hot coals must have happened fairly often on every ship that cooked. If this were not noticed because the men were busy elsewhere or if a blaze got out of control, the ship might have to be abandoned. Or so much water might be applied to put out the fire, it could sink the ship.

A great deal of wine was transported by ship, and drunkenness aboard must have been very common. Alcohol does not mix well with sailing.

6. Sometimes merchant ships were deliberately sunk by warships (who first replenished their stores) to cut an enemy's supply lines or to prevent the news of a warship's existence in the area from becoming known. Pirates did the same but with less patriotic motives; their objective was to loot the cargo and make slaves of the crew. There would be less evidence and trouble if the victim ship simply disappeared at sea; it might be weeks before anyone would discover it was missing. So they would smash a hole in the bottom and let the ship fill with water and drop from sight.

On some occasions, shipowners have been known to do the same thing to their own ships—after insuring ship and cargo as heavily as possible.

7. Finally, there are quite a number of rather exotic ways in which ships can be sunk. The statistical chances seem very low, but the fact is that several small ships a year go down as a result of freak mishaps, and our period of interest covers a great many years. For example, a sudden sleet storm in the Black Sea could ice up mast and yards and cause a ship to capsize; this is a common accident in northern waters and there are winters every few hundred years cold enough to freeze the Bosporus.

Large single waves have been known to rise up suddenly from a relatively calm sea and sink unsuspecting fishing craft that were riding easily with their hatches open. Nearly every old fisherman has encountered one or two of these solitary waves in his lifetime. Fishing craft in modern times have been known to sink themselves by loading too much fish aboard; they head for port with the after-deck awash, and sometimes they do not make it.

All the above reasons why sailing ships sank in deep water were valid from ancient times until about a century ago. Since the causes of deepwater losses remained the same, we can make use of statistics gathered in the eighteenth and nineteenth centuries A.D. to get the approximate number of ships lost two thousand years earlier.

In the mid eighteen hundreds the British Board of Trade kept good statistics on ship losses in the waters surrounding the British Isles and each year published a wreck chart. Peter Throckmorton has kindly furnished a copy of the one for 1869, which is marked with hundreds of dots—each representing a wreck—so that the shore line looks as though it were sprouting dozens of fence lines, each extending many miles out to sea. It shows that well over two hundred ships went down well offshore during that year in the North Sea, Irish Sea, and English Channel.

The Board of Trade also published statistics on the kinds and causes of wrecks for the previous ten years, beginning with the types of ships lost. About 7 per cent were fishing boats, 27 per cent were colliers, 19 per cent were carrying stone or ores, and 47 per cent had other cargoes or were in ballast. About half those

ships (including nearly all the colliers) were in coastal trade, and
the other half were lost while crossing one of the seas or the channel.

In those ten years, 2,537 ships sank well out at sea. This is
roughly comparable to ten times the loss rate of "over two
hundred" for 1869, and it suggests that the average losses in the
waters offshore of the British Isles in the nineteen hundreds were
about two hundred and fifty ships a year, or twenty-five thousand
per century. Actually those waters are not deep (generally they
do not exceed a hundred meters) because the whole area is part
of the European coastal shelf, but at similar distances offshore
of the Mediterranean countries, the water could be very deep.

Table 4. **Causes of Wrecks Resulting in Total Loss (Other than Collisions) on Waters near the United Kingdom**

Year	Stress of Weather	Inattention, Carelessness, Neglect	Defects in Ship or Equipment	Various Causes	Causes Unknown
1859	298	84	42	70	33
1860	278	103	49	40	6
1861	302	89	48	49	25
1862	242	72	25	96	20
1863	332	61	31	65	14
1864	163	89	39	64	31
1865	245	99	38	61	27
1866	276	125	74	68	19
1867	385	106	65	84	16
1868	265	87	71	85	19
	2786	915	482	682	210
			Total Ships Lost:		5075

The Board of Trade statistics also note that of those ships lost
to "stress of weather" (principally wind) in 1871, more than half
went down at wind velocities of force six and under, "when the
wind did not exceed a strong breeze and a ship could still carry
single reefs and top gallant sails." Only 30 per cent of the wind-
stressed ships were lost in strong gales and hurricanes. Thus, a really violent storm is not required to sink a ship.

Almost 10 per cent of these ships were nearly new; 38 per cent were less than fifteen years old; 34 per cent were fifteen to thirty years old; and 18 per cent were older than thirty years, with several dozen ships aged sixty to a hundred years old.

As for the size of the lost ships (1871 statistics), 42 per cent were under a hundred tons; 36 per cent were a hundred to three hundred tons; 14 per cent were three to six hundred tons; and 8 per cent were over six hundred tons. Translating tonnage into length in very rough terms: a tublike wooden sailing ship of a hundred tons could be less than twenty-five meters long; one of three hundred tons, less than thirty-five meters; and one of six hundred tons, less than forty-five meters.

Now one last set of statistics for the sailing-ship buffs who may read this. Eleven per cent of the 1871 ships lost were steamships and 26 per cent were schooners (both of which could move well into the wind). This means that although 37 per cent had a huge advantage over the ancient square-sail ships, they went down anyway. The somewhat lesser advantage of more modern rigging and construction was enjoyed by the 15 per cent brigs, 12 per cent barques, 11 per cent brigantines, and the other miscellaneous sail types that went down in that average year of nineteenth-century trade.

Statistics on sinkings, however useful they may be to one concerned with the number of ships lost in deep water, do not give an adequate mental picture of how the losses occurred. Therefore, a few specific examples of how sailing ships have been lost in the twentieth century and of how modern steel ships are still lost in the Mediterranean may give a better insight into why the ancient ships went down.

For example, H.M.S. *Eurydice,* moving up the English Channel under all plain sail at the end of a four-month cruise to the West Indies, stood close inshore to signal her safe arrival. Watchers on the cliffs at Spithead, admiring the *Eurydice* and the *Emma,* which followed it, noted that the glass was falling rapidly and that there was an "ominous stillness" as the west wind decreased. At ten minutes to four, the wind suddenly veered to the east. Both ships disappeared into a snow squall with violent east winds. By four o'clock, the cloud bank lifted again but now, to the amazement of the distant observers, the *Eurydice* had disappeared and the *Emma* continued on as before. In those few minutes, a ship had vanished into the sea. The *Emma* picked up five men of the 368 aboard the *Eurydice,* who reported that one sudden, violent blast had blown the ship over so that it filled with water through open ventilators and sank.

The sailing ships that survived into this century were the product of five thousand years of development. Most were steel, over a hundred meters long, had three or four masts, and carried square as well as fore-and-aft sails. These sail training ships were as well built and as well sailed as any in history, yet they, too, were subject to sea disasters as were their distant ancestors.

In July of 1932 the German training ship *Niobe* had an experience similar to that of *Eurydice* while operating not far from its home port of Kiel. A sudden line squall capsized it and although this time there were no open ports, it sank in four minutes—before boats could be launched.

The Belgian training ship *Comte de Smet de Nayer* headed south across the Bay of Biscay bound for Madeira. She was running before a strong wind when a leak developed in the forward hold; the water kept steadily rising even though hand pumps were used to supplement the steam pump. Eventually all the sails were cut away but even then the wind pressure on the masts kept the ship driving into the sea and forcing more water through the hole. It became evident the situation was hopeless but it was impossible to lower the boats properly because of the forward motion. Finally one boat was launched upright and the cadets were ordered to jump overboard and swim for it. Twenty-six were saved, but the senior officers went down with the ship as tradition demanded; the cause of the leak was never determined.

A graceful four-masted steel barque was the *Admiral Karp-fanger,* used by the Hamburg-Amerika line to train officer cadets. She sailed from Australia in February 1938 with a cargo of 42,500 bags of wheat and a total crew of sixty men. This ship had modern equipment and was fresh from overhaul; thirty-two days out it reported by radio, and then—nothing.

Of the one hundred and thirty vessels that left European ports for the Pacific in the summer of 1905, fifty-three had vanished in Cape Horn waters by the end of July.

The Danish ship *København* was a splendid five-master of thirty-nine hundred tons bound for Melbourne. It last reported its position by radio, on December 22, 1928, as several hundred miles east of Tristan da Cunha, after which all radio signals ceased. To this day, no one knows what happened, although there were guesses that the ballast had shifted, that it struck an iceberg, or that a sudden squall caught it with all sails set.

The most recent loss of an auxiliary training ship was the four-masted barque *Pamir,* en route from Argentina to Germany in September 1957. The ship encountered hurricane Carrie somewhere south of the Azores, and its cargo of grain (improperly stowed by conscript soldiers during a stevedore strike) shifted. Through heavy radio interference came a series of ever more ominous messages: "Foremast broken by heavy seas," "All sails lost," "Listing 45 degrees, in danger of sinking." Eventually, five survivors were picked up in a swamped and split lifeboat. The explanation given for the loss was that "a sudden veering of the wind in the center of the hurricane caused the sails to beat back and cause serious damage to the rigging and further damage to the hull by falling pieces of rigging."

Small ships, more nearly the size of the ancient ones, are still lost at a remarkably high rate. For example, a news dispatch from Tokyo datelined April 2, 1972, reported thirty-three small ships sunk or capsized in the waters around Japan in three days of squalls and high winds. Small shipping companies and fisheries were accused of kamikaze (suicide) practices because they sent the ships to sea in the face of adverse weather forecasts.

An astonishing number of modern steel ships will disappear at sea this year. Even in these days of careful inspection by insurance companies, no pirates, radioed weather broadcasts, and voyages measured in a few days instead of weeks, some will be declared to be "missing without a trace." No one can ever be sure why those ships were lost.

In a piece by John Fairhall in the Manchester *Guardian* of June 22, 1971, he reported that seventy ships were "missing" in the previous ten years out of 2,766 ships lost. The total was made up of various categories: foundered, burned, collided, wrecked, lost for other reasons, and missing. Wrecked was the largest category (1,136 ships). Next was foundered; 771 ships were overwhelmed by the sea alone, without the aid of rocks, reefs, or other ships. Many of these foundered ships, which represent one fourth of all those lost, are down in deep water and would be suitable deep-search objects. But the "missing" category (2.5 per cent of the total) is of even greater interest to us here.

Lloyd's of London posts a ship as "missing" if it disappears without known cause, leaving no survivors and no substantial wreckage. "Posted as missing" is the formal death certificate of the crew and the clearance for the insurance claim to be paid.

Now consider a few recent "missings" in the Mediterranean from the files of Jim Dawson, a well-known Lloyd's broker. These give one the flavor of the circumstances leading up to the "posted as missing" decision.

The *Hedia,* a Liberian steamer of 2,434 gross tons with a crew of twenty was bound for Venice carrying four thousand tons of bulk phosphate. The last radio report from the ship, on March 14, 1962, said it had encountered violent gales and heavy seas south of Sicily but that all was well. Life belts and a hatchway with the name were picked up off the island of Lampedusa a week later.

El Arish, a motor vessel owned by the government of Egypt, disappeared a day or two after November 17, 1965. She was bound from London for Piraeus and Alexandria with a cargo of two thousand tons of steel, two hundred and eighty tons of lead ingots, and some machinery. The ship had reported some storm damage and intended to put into port for repairs but was never heard from again.

Hashlosha, of Haifa, an Israeli motor vessel with eighteen hundred tons of clay in bulk from Kimlos Island for Marseilles sent a *m'aidez* (May Day) on January 24, 1967, as its last contact with the shore. It was believed to be eighty miles west of Naples in an area lashed by gales. Two overturned lifeboats were picked up off Sardinia on the twenty-seventh.

Oostmeep, a Dutch ship with a cargo of steel billets from Brussels for Monfalcone, on the Adriatic Sea, reported passing Gibraltar on October 29, 1968; it was last seen off Cape Bougaroni on the thirty-first. This 1,134-gross-ton ship had been recently surveyed, and the only suggestion as to why it was lost was that there were gale-force winds and generally heavy seas in the lower Adriatic. Nothing more. A new steel ship, well manned, simply disappeared.

Kiki, a Cyprus steamer carrying five thousand tons of coke from Poland to Yugoslavia, reported itself in distress on February 3, 1971, with the following cryptic message: "Request help, SOS, water's entered in." No position was given, but British planes from Malta searched along the route the vessel was expected to take without finding a trace.

The above stories produce a mental picture of ships unexpectedly getting into trouble in the Mediterranean, mostly from storms, and suddenly disappearing. Most of these "missings" seem likely to have "foundered"—that is, they were overwhelmed by the sea, took on water, and sank. If the statistics previously cited for all oceans hold good in the Mediterranean—that is, 771 foundered for seventy missing—the ratio of foundering (with some survivors) to missings (with no survivors) is about 11:1.

That means for the five large ships just cited as missing in the Mediterranean (undoubtedly there were more) fifty-five more foundered, or a total of sixty ships went down in deep water in a ten-year period. This is equivalent to six hundred in a century or six thousand in a thousand-year period. The small craft—fishing boats, yachts, ferries, etc., which are much harder to get statistics on—must have been lost in far greater numbers.

Anyone who still has any doubts about the kinds of troubles ships can get into at sea need only read the following paragraph on the subject. This is the "Perils" paragraph of the American Institute Hull Clauses, dated January 18, 1970, commonly used in insuring modern ships at sea.

Perils

Touching the Adventures and Perils which the Underwriters are contented to bear and take upon themselves, they are of the Seas, Men-of-War, Fire, Lightning, Earthquake, Enemies, Pirates, Rovers, Assailing Thieves, Jettisons, Letters of Mart and Counter Mart, Surprisals, Takings at Sea, Arrests, Restraints and Detainments

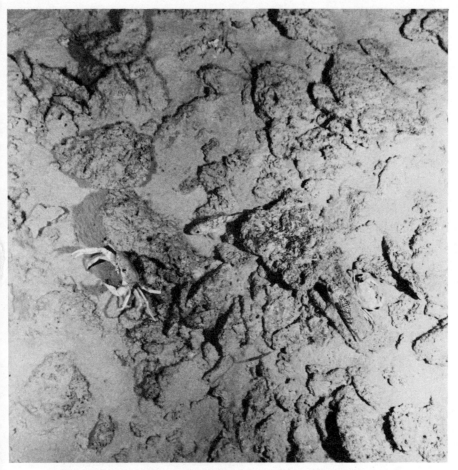

6. Small crabs and fish inhabit this deep reef (about four hundred meters, or twelve hundred feet) southwest of the Florida Keys. The circumstances surrounding the taking of this photo by the *Alcoa Seaprobe* are described in the text. (*Glenn Tillman*)

7. The *Oceaneer* is of the same type but a little smaller than the 40-meter (120-foot) supply boat recommended as an advance survey boat and small-object salvage vessel for use in depths to about five hundred meters, or fifteen hundred feet. (*Ocean Science & Engineering, Inc.*)

8. The J-Star being lowered over the side of the *Oceaneer* to salvage the major pieces of a 727 that crashed in one thousand feet of water on take-off from Los Angeles International Airport. (*Ocean Science & Engineering, Inc.*)

9. CURV III (Controlled Underwater Recovery Vehicle), built by the Naval Undersea Center for the retrieval of torpedoes and small objects from depths to six thousand feet. (*H. Talkington, U.S.N.*)

10. Controls for CURV III are in a portable van that can be shipped by air as a complete package, with the vehicle and its cable, to the part of the world where its services are needed. (*H. Talkington, U.S.N.*)

of all Kings, Princes and Peoples, of what nation, condition or quality soever, Barratry of the Master and Mariners and of all other like Perils, Losses and Misfortunes that have or shall come to the Hurt, Detriment or Damage of the Vessel, or any part thereof, excepting, however, such of the foregoing perils as may be excluded by provisions elsewhere in the Policy or by endorsement thereon.

The history of the Columbine class of vessels as reported by Peter Throckmorton in his book *Shipwrecks and Archaeology* is most instructive in the study of ship losses. H.M.S. *Columbine* was a sloop of war, brig-rigged as a general-purpose ship. Over a hundred like her were built in the early eighteen hundreds. They were a hundred feet long at deck level, built of oak, nailed and sheathed in copper to keep borers away. A hundred and twenty-one men sailed her, although a quarter of that number would have done for a merchantman of the same size. These were stout ships, well sailed by disciplined crews, yet the statistics on their loss are a good indication of how dangerous it was to be a sailor in those days.

Of the seventy Columbine-class ships built between 1803 and 1809, nineteen were lost by mishap. Of these, six foundered with all hands. Gilley's *Narratives of Shipwrecks of the Royal Navy* then lists another nineteen ships of the class lost at sea, of which eight foundered in deep water with all hands and the rest ran into various rocks and shores around the world. If those numbers are correct, and a total of fourteen ships foundered out of eighty-nine total, then the percentage lost offshore, presumably in deep water, is 15.8. That number tells a lot about the risk of losing a ship only a hundred and fifty years ago.

Gilley also covers the period between 1793 and 1850, listing 372 naval ships lost by "mishap." Of these, nearly half were lost by running onto unmarked shoals or rocks and another seventy-eight foundered in gales at sea, usually with all hands. Another dozen were lost by fire—always a danger on a wooden ship with open cooking fires, lanterns, and candles, especially in the presence of gunpowder. Navies less disciplined than the British lost proportionately more ships to fire; the Turks lost entire fleets which caught fire and blew up—with and without help from their enemies. In any case, seventy-eight ships went down in gales and twelve were lost to fire out of 372 total; this means at least 24 per cent sunk in what could have been deep water.

During the Napoleonic wars, which lasted twenty-two years, the Royal Navy lost over three hundred ships by mishap but fewer than a dozen by enemy action. This is at a time when the total of vessels in the Navy was about two hundred and fifty; the figures suggest that the fleet was completely rebuilt every twenty years if the entire shipbuilding program only replaced lost ships.

Relying on Lloyd's statistics once more—this time for merchant ships in the last days of sail, when ships were probably better designed, built, and sailed than ever before—we have the following shocker: In the five years from 1864 to 1869, ten thousand sailing ships insured in England were lost in various parts of the world, nearly a thousand without a trace! Fifteen hundred men drowned out of the three hundred thousand that were at sea each year. The numbers suggest that in the eighteen hundreds about half of all working sailing ships were wrecked or lost and that the other half eventually were scrapped as unseaworthy.

To recapitulate the results of the rather spotty statistics above and throughout this book, it appears that of all the ships ever built in the world, over 95 per cent were wooden sailing ships. Of these, about half were wrecked, nearly 80 per cent of which ran aground or had some other shallow-water mishaps. The remainder, over 20 per cent, were lost well out at sea in accidents not connected with a shore line. They sank in whatever depth existed there—which, in most of the world, is likely to be deep. This means that approximately 10 per cent of all the seagoing ships ever built left their hulls on the deep-sea bottom.

If we take the above statistics on sailing-ship losses in the eighteenth to nineteenth centuries A.D. and apply them to the estimates of the number of ships built in ancient times it would appear that at least 15,500 merchant ships sank in the first millennium B.C. alone. For the whole period of ancient times, the number could be forty thousand ships down in deep water.

This fraction of the ancient ships is the target of the deepwater archaeologist.

CHAPTER VI

Shallow-Water Marine Archaeology

Marine archaeology can be said to have begun in 1900, when a party of sponge divers accidentally found an ancient wreck and were then recruited by the Greek Government to salvage statues from it. The beginning was crude and destructive of much historical material, yet it aroused world-wide scholarly interest in antiquities under the sea.

The first fifty years was characterized by sporadic accidental discoveries, vandalism and looting of wrecks, archaeologists waiting topside for whatever the divers brought up, and little public interest in anything except statuary. The big change of recent years came with the invention of convenient self-contained underwater breathing apparatus, which permits archaeologists to go below and do the work themselves. This chapter reviews the development of modern methods by sketching the most important and interesting wreck excavations.

The purpose of retelling these familiar stories here is not only to give proper credit to the great men of underwater archaeology but to underline the differences between the work done in the past and that which is now proposed for deep water.

Here then are the accounts in chronological order of the wrecks that are mainly responsible for the present status of marine archaeology.

Antikythera

At the southern tip of the Peloponnesus is Cape Malea, around which all ships passed as they headed southwest into the Mediterranean. Not far off the cape is the large island of Kythera. Both these rocky promontories were surrounded by rough waters and tricky currents, so sailors tended to give them a wide berth. Midway between Kythera and the western tip of Crete, some fifty miles away, is a much smaller island: Antikythera, well situated to intercept ships running before the northeast wind at night.

The little island also could serve as a shelter from winds from the other direction, and so it was that in the fall of 1900 a Greek sponge boat returning from Africa took shelter from a southerly storm in the quiet lee of its steep cliffs. After a day or two of boredom, the captain, Dimitrios Kondos, decided to send a man down to see if there were sponges in the area. The undersea slope was steep, and although the boat was close in to the cliff, the diver first touched bottom at thirty fathoms (sixty meters). He had been on the bottom only a few minutes when he blew himself to the surface in a fright and told a wild tale of a city below populated by men, women, horses—their features eaten away as though by syphilis.

Captain Kondos scoffed and made the next dive himself; when he surfaced again, he carried the arm of a bronze statue. He had found a wreck that lay on the narrow ledge parallel to the cliff face; below that, the bottom sloped steeply into deep water. The divers recognized that the ancient ship might be valuable, so they stayed at the site for several days, each making several short dives a day and recovering such artifacts as they could easily break off or dislodge. When the weather eased, they sailed for home. The stories vary on whether they tried to sell some of the salvaged pieces and were turned in to the police or whether in a burst of patriotism they immediately reported the find to the Greek Government. Anyway, the story of the find was soon out and it led to great public excitement.

By the end of November, Captain Kondos and his crew were

back at the site, accompanied by Professor A. Economou of the university at Athens and Minister of Education Spiridon Stais, who had arranged funds and a navy support ship. The divers had agreed to raise the rest of the statues if they were paid properly and given the use of a winch. Unknowingly, they had offered to do the deepest salvage job in history up to that time. In the first few days, they raised the philosopher's head, a bronze sword, and parts of various statues.

There were headlines about archaeological treasures, for as Peter Throckmorton points out, the country was naturally proud that Greek divers were raising Greek antiquities that had been taken long before by a Roman conquerer. Later the godlike "athlete," a very lifelike majestic bronze statue of a naked man with porcelain eyes and calm demeanor, was recovered.

The divers poked in the bottom with rods to find objects, which were then attached to the winch cable. Not surprisingly, many statues broke as the winch dragged them free of the mud, but the pile of marble statues on deck grew, though most of them were badly eaten by borers. After six months of exhausting work, all the small, loose objects had been recovered. These included blue glass bowls, a gold brooch of Eros, tiles, pottery, a bronze bed, human bones, and, of course, amphorae. When they left, the divers reported that they thought there were other statues still at the site.

The age and origin of the wreck was a subject of long debate, because the bronzes were from the fourth century B.C. while some of the pottery seemed to be first century. A radiocarbon date on some of the wood gave 120 B.C. ± forty years. But the ultimate evidence was the setting on the clockwork "computer," which precisely put the date at 82 B.C. and suggested the statues were part of General Sulla's booty en route to Rome.

Mahdia

In 1907 Alfred Merlin, then a director of antiquities for the Tunisian Government, was browsing in a bazaar when he noticed a small, bronze, lime-encrusted figurine in one of the stalls. It was much like some he had seen in the Louvre, but it seemed to have been recently found beneath the sea. He acquired the piece for the museum and questioned the apprehensive shopkeeper about its origin. He learned it had been found by Greek sponge divers near the coastal town of Mahdia and set off at once on camelback to find out more. After some initial reluctance, Merlin persuaded a diver to show him the site of the wreck. He then obtained the assistance of a French Navy tug, raised the money to pay the divers, and in a few days was ready to go.

After eight days of searching, the wreck was found—sixty marble columns, weighing over two hundred tons, in water forty meters deep. No statues were to be seen, but there was wood beneath the columns. The divers then lifted and moved the columns to enter what seemed to be the muddy interior of the ship. Even though the mud was only a few centimeters thick, it had helped to protect the treasures beneath, and traces of paint still remained on the wood of the hull. Marble statues like those that had fared badly on the Antikythera wreck shone like new when they were washed down on deck. There were also busts in bronze, candelabra, kraters for mixing wine, and pieces of many statues.

As the divers worked, Merlin pondered the origin of the ship and how and when it came to be wrecked at that site. One clue to the date of the wreck came from a small terra cotta lamp of a design that had been popular for a short time at the end of the second century B.C. Based on the markings on the statuary and a stele from Piraeus, he decided the origin of the voyage was probably Athens. As for the owner of the ship, his first guess was that it was Roman loot, possibly from Sulla's campaign of 80 B.C. Later, however, Merlin decided that the sculptures were not originals but copies made for the extensive art trade of that time. His opinion was that thousands of shiploads of such statues, columns, decorated furniture, and jewelry had been exported from Greece to Italy.

The wreck was more than three miles from shore. Since its columns occupied a space thirty meters by ten, the corbita was a fair-sized ship—or it was very much overloaded. Apparently, it had been driven many days before a northeast storm to have gotten so far off course—or perhaps its intended port was on the African coast. Disabled, possibly by losing rudder or mast, the ship had been overwhelmed by the sea. It went down quickly and landed right side up on the bottom, with the deck cargo still in place. The wooden parts that projected above the seabed were rapidly destroyed, but the mud preserved the rest. Probably, the Mahdia wreck behaved almost exactly as a ship would have that went down in deeper water; it is a good model for one to think about.

The excavation lasted five seasons, until 1913, by which time the art works filled six rooms of the El Alaoui Museum in Tunis.

The statuary includes a bronze statue of "the spirit of the games" and a "Herm" of Dionysus with a long beard, both signed by Boethus of Chalcedon. Other statues included Aphrodite, Artemis, Athena, and a winged Eros. There are bedsteads, inlays, and two-handled wine kraters as tall as a man, decorated with pictures of Bacchus. The columns turned out to be a complete prefabricated temple. This great find caused Salomon Reinach, an archaeologist-philosopher, to speak of the Mediterranean as "the treasure vault of the ancient world."

Cape Artemision

In the foyer of the great hall of the United Nations in New York, a great, naked god of bronze is poised, about to throw a trident or a thunderbolt at some luckless being. This heroic Zeus or Poseidon from the golden age of Greece is a copy of what may be the greatest work of ancient statuary in existence. It has survived only because it was lost beneath the sea for two thousand years. Probably it was part of a shipload of loot, because, near this fifth-century-B.C. figure, an exquisite third-century bronze statue of a jockey boy was found, along with about half of his bronze horse.

The wreck was found not far from Cape Artemision in 1927 by a sponge diver who had descended to free a trawl that had snagged on the bottom. The diver was astonished to find the net caught by the arm of a god reaching up through the sea bottom. But he wrenched off the arm and took it to Professor George Karo of the German Archaeological Institute in Athens. After some bargaining, it was agreed that he would show the location of the wreck to an expedition supported by Alexander Benaki, a wealthy cotton merchant and patron of the arts.

The water depth at the wreck is about a hundred and forty feet, and very little of the old ship projected above the muddy sea floor. However, two statues mentioned above were found, along with wooden pieces of the ship, all protected by the mud. The salvage operation was making good progress when one of the divers decided to demonstrate his contempt for the decompression tables by inflating his suit with air and quickly blowing himself to the surface. He immediately died of an embolism and the work was abandoned. The exact location of the wreck was lost.

That is the approximate story—there are a number of variations. Nothing competent seems to have been published on the find in any language, and most of the original participants are now dead. In 1930, Dr. George Milonas, a classical archaeologist, made an attempt to find the wreck with helmet divers, but he was unsuccessful. If other divers have tried in recent years, there is no official record.

With patience and modern technology, it is surely possible to find that wreck again. Almost certainly, there are more statues there that were selected by the same tasteful person who chose the god and the jockey. If a modern patron of the arts chose to invest, say a hundred thousand dollars, in a search, he would have a reasonably good chance of finding more million-dollar statues and becoming the hero of the world of art. Any statues found would, of course, join the first ones in the National Archaeological Museum at Athens.

Grand Congloue

A chain of small islands juts from the blue sea a few miles southwest of Marseilles, France, the easternmost of which is Grand Congloue. Many a sailing ship approaching that harbor at night or in a storm must have narrowly missed the steep, barren rock. Some did not, and among them, in the second century B.C., was the huge cargo ship of Marcus Sextius. This ship may have displaced as much as eight hundred tons and carried ten thousand amphorae—although there remains some disagreement about the size and whether or not this find may possibly have been two ships sunk at the same spot, one atop the other.

The present legend began when Frédéric Dumas visited the hospital bed of an expert salvage diver who had been paralyzed by the bends. The crippled diver told him a special secret: the location of a huge colony of lobsters living amid old clay pots at the foot of a steep cliff. Pots instantly signaled the possibility of an old wreck to Dumas, and he told Captain J.-Y. Cousteau at once. The year was 1952, and by coincidence Cousteau's ship *Calypso* was just about ready to leave Marseilles for the Red Sea, with archaeologist Fernand Benoit aboard, on an expedition to examine some sites believed to be old wrecks.

They decided to have a look at the lobster pots of Grand Congloue first. Dumas made the first dive, recognized some underwater landmarks his diver friend had described, but saw no old pots. Then Cousteau went down twenty-five fathoms through the blue gloom to a bed of sand and rubble at the base of the cliff. He had almost reached the end of his diving time when he saw a single amphora, then a mound and bits of rubble. He grabbed a promising-looking clump and a bronze hook; then he headed upward.

At the surface, Professor Benoit quickly identified the clump as second-century-B.C. Campanian-ware cups stuck together with lime deposits. There was no doubt that the *Calypso* was over an important ancient wreck. Cousteau's voyage was over on the day it started; his fifteen divers went to work at once to bring up the dishes and amphorae that lay almost in their own front yard. The wreck mound readily yielded hundreds of pieces of pottery, but as they dug downward, the soft mud gave way to more consolidated sediments and the digging slowed. The summer weather gave way to wind, rough seas and cold water. It was not a good place to anchor a ship, and so the expedition ingeniously devised a derrick on the edge of the cliff to handle the airlift hose that was used to excavate the main part of the ship.

In the beginning, they estimated that the excavation might take two years—but in the end it was closer to ten. By the time the site was abandoned, over eight thousand amphorae and twelve thousand pieces of mass-produced dinnerware were brought to the surface, both of which created something of a storage problem. The divers also found the ship's anchor and lead pipes that possibly were part of a bilge-pump system.

The diving produced many artifacts, but the real archaeology was done at the surface when the finders tried to unravel the history of the ship. Where had it come from? Who owned it? What year was it wrecked? The best evidence came from the amphorae, most of which were of two distinctly different kinds.

The upper, more recently loaded amphorae, were tall and slender with a volume of five liters. They were stamped with the letters L. TITI and it was soon deduced that these carried wines from the vineyards of Lucius Titius who lived between Rome and Naples.

The lower amphorae were short and plump, held twenty-two liters each, and were marked SES followed by a trident or an anchor. Significantly, they turned out to be some seventy years older than the ones above. Since the writings of Titus Livy, a Roman historian, mention a shipowner and wine merchant named Marcus Sextius who lived on the Greek island of Delos in the middle of the third century B.C., Cousteau decided to go there and look for further clues. In an old section of the city where large villas of the rich had once stood, he found a mosaic floor whose central pattern was a trident with S's between the three tines, much like the markings on the amphorae. The villa seemed never to have been completed, leading to speculation that the sinking of the great ship at Congloue had bankrupted M. Sextius.

The work of Cousteau, Benoit, Dumas, and the others at Congloue was pioneering. They were inventive and persistent, and tried out a lot of new ideas. Although free-diving equipment had been used on wrecks before 1952, this was its first massive archaeological use. Underwater television was used to watch and direct divers. The airlift system was used on a grand scale to move mud and bring up artifacts. Finally, they carried the work to completion although, after a few years of diving in cold water, it must have lost much of its glamour.

Spargi

The sea bottom between Corsica and Sardinia is rough and rocky. Here and there these rocks make small islands and dangerous reefs. In 1939 an Italian navy diver named Mozza was repairing the anchor chains of a lighted marker buoy off the isle of Spargi when he discovered an amphora field. He brought up several to prove his claim but, because of some mix-up in recording the depth of the wreck, subsequent divers did not find it; furthermore there was insufficient interest at the time to make a serious search. Much later, in 1957, a visiting journalist named Gianni Roghi heard the story and in one hour of diving with SCUBA equipment found the wreck in only eighteen meters of water.

The old ship's bottom had been ripped open by the shallow reef and it had continued on just far enough to sink at a depth that afforded it protection from the waves. There were thousands of amphorae (three thousand, eventually) as well as plates and bowls from the ship's galley. Roghi and his associates showed samples of the finds to Professors Lamboglia and Miro Mirabella, who watch over antique finds from the sea in behalf of the Italian Government. They were particularly interested in the report that the wood of the hull could be felt under a layer of amphorae. An expedition was planned, and by May of 1958 they were back at the site.

This was to be a precise excavation, for it was clear that there had been very little disturbance of this wreck. The top layer, of a hundred and twenty amphorae, had become disordered, but below that the jugs were in exactly their original position, nested and precisely aligned. Around the perimeter, Roghi drove iron stakes at two-meter intervals in such a way that he could stretch yellow plastic tape between them to make a grid. Then each square was marked with a number so that it was possible to take a vertical photograph of each square and to number the location of each amphora.

As the excavation progressed, they found a bronze lamp, a

green glass jar with gold decorations, the ship's temple, and hundreds more Campanian dishes and cups, looking much as when they had been packed. Professor Lamboglia was able to set the date of the wreck at between 120 and 100 B.C. Some of the dishes were in use by the crew of the ship, for two were stuck together by the remains of a meal.

Digging deeper, the divers now came to the wood of the ship. Enough of the outline was exposed so that a plan could be made. It was solidly built, about thirty meters long, ten wide, and with a cargo capacity of a hundred and fifty to two hundred tons. Much of the outside was sheathed in lead with a high silver content.

Apparently this excavation was never quite completed because funds ran out. The ship's owner and origin were never discovered, but much was learned and it was another step forward in shallow-water archaeology.

Cape Gelidonya

In order fully to appreciate the finding and excavation in 1960 of this bronze-age wreck on the south coast of Turkey, one should read the writings of Peter Throckmorton, who was largely responsible for its beginnings. His books best capture the spirit of the Turkish sponge divers who first told him of the wreck at Cape Gelidonya; for generations, these brave and rugged men of the sponge trade have passed down the secret locations of the best sponge beds and of the places where amphora mounds can be found that supply water jugs for the diving boats.

Throckmorton's method for finding old wrecks was straightforward. He would visit the waterfront bars of coastal towns, pleasantly engage divers in shop talk over a powerful drink called raki, and eventually turn the conversation to "old pots in the sea." Every diver knew places where one could find the old pots—amphorae—and other things too. Such things as lead from ancient anchors or bronze from old tools; these were, until recently, sold to junk dealers for scrap value. With patience, much time at sea on the diving boats, and a lot of raki, Throckmorton began mapping the dozens of old wrecks the divers showed him along that deserted coast. Always he sought some special one that would make archaeologists really sit up and take notice.

Eventually during a long raki session in 1958, his old friend and sponge-boat skipper, Captain Kemal, asked how one would go about dynamiting some flat bronze ingots he knew about to get them free of the sea bottom. The ingots, he said, were "rotten." Previously, he had salvaged some knives, a spear point, and a hatchet of bronze but they were not strong and broke when the children played with them.

Clearly this was a very old wreck (bronze knives meant before 1000 B.C.), and so, in a reckless moment, the chronically broke Throckmorton offered Kemal double the scrap value if he would hold off dynamiting the wreck until it had been seen by archaeologists.

By Christmas that year, he had returned to New York and enlisted the help of George Bass, then a research assistant at the University of Pennsylvania Museum. They agreed to do a precise underwater excavation together, uncompromisingly following land standards, and set about raising funds and locating equipment. By May of 1959 they had an expedition on the site at Cape Gelidonya; George Bass was the director, Throckmorton the technical adviser.

The main problem was to plot the location of each piece exactly, so that when the excavation was finished it would be possible to reconstruct the position each piece had come from. A whole series of ingenious devices for measuring, drawing, photographing, tagging, lifting, and surveying were employed under difficult conditions. The party camped on a narrow shingle beach at the base of a steep cliff from which rocks fell at random moments, and so they were literally between a landslide and the deep blue sea.

The material they found showed that the ship was about contemporaneous with the Trojan War (1200 B.C.) or with the time of the mysterious Sea People.

There were important finds of tools (hammers, chisels, axes, adzes, awls, knives, and plowshares) that were not unlike the ones used in Turkey today except that they were made of bronze instead of steel. Some of these had incised letters in the still-undeciphered Cypro-Minoan script used on Cyprus in the late

Bronze Age. The sea diggers also found bronze blanks for making more tools, and these led to the theory that the ship was in the business of trading new tools for old, which were then repaired and sold at the next stop. The oxhide-shaped bronze ingots were the important find. The oxhide shape is sort of a webbed X, about eighty centimeters in the longer direction, three centimeters thick, and weighing some 25 kilograms.

Forty of them, twenty-seven with founding marks, almost certainly had come from the copper mines of Cyprus. There were also bits of treasure such as a black cylinder seal five hundred years older than the wreck, a Syrian scarab, a mass of blue and white Phoenician beads, and three almost complete sets of scale weights. A fragment of a basket made of matting and rope was found between two copper ingots, indicating that very delicate fibers can survive beneath the sea if the conditions are right. Enough of the wood remained to give a cross section of the ship, whose hull planks had been held down by ballast stones above which were brushwood padding and a mass of ingots.

The Gelidonya wreck artifacts that survived three thousand years of difficult, shallow-water conditions hint at the possibilities that may exist in the deep.

Yassi Ada

A dozen miles west of Bodrum, Turkey, is a small, flat island: Yassi Ada. Extending seaward from it, a reef about a meter deep forms a ship trap. Ships running down the ragged west coast of Turkey, threading their way between the rocks and islands and mindful of a lee shore on the Greek island of Cos only a few miles dead ahead, would shorten their route a bit by cutting close to shore on the inside of each turn. Those that cut too close to Yassi Ada were caught in the trap. The shoal would have been screened by waves, so a ship running before the wind would have had no warning. On striking this undersea rock a ship would tear its own bottom out in one grating, grinding crash. The mast would snap and the sailors would be flung onto the deck. The only question remaining was how much farther the ship would drive before its wounded hulk would go down. Over the years more than twenty ships sank immediately in water shallow enough to be reached by divers. Others continued on for some distance before going to the bottom in deeper water.

It was to Yassi Ada that Captain Kemal and his sponge divers took Peter Throckmorton in 1958, thinking it a little strange that anyone would be so interested in old, broken pots and ancient junk. South of the reef the bottom was strewn with shards of cooking pots and wreckage; at seventeen fathoms there was a mass of amphorae. There were over a dozen wrecks, which eventually had to be given numbers so the archaeologists could agree on which one they were discussing.

Somewhat later, in reprisal for dismissing the relative of a Turkish official, Throckmorton was refused permission to re-enter the country, so George Bass and the University of Pennsylvania group proceeded to Bodrum and Yassi Ada after their success at Cape Gelidonya.

From the selection of wrecks at Yassi Ada, Bass chose wreck three, which turned out to be an early Byzantine ship. The wreck was about twenty meters long and lay on a gentle slope at a depth of thirty-two meters. The first summer, 1961, was spent in precisely mapping the surface layer; every amphora, broken or whole, had its shape, exact orientation, and position recorded.

Fragments of wood were examined by Frederick van Doorninck, who plotted the position and angle of every nail hole and scored mark. In the end this extreme care and patience paid off. The party was able to date the ship, define the area of its origin, the kinds of jobs the crew filled, the cargo, the cooking arrangements, the way the ship was assembled, and the captain's name (Georgios, Senior).

Actual finds of artifacts included some nine hundred amphorae (but only a hundred stoppers), some of which were coated with resin inside. Since the ship was headed toward a large wine-producing area, probably the amphorae had been new and empty. There were also twenty-four oil lamps aboard, many kinds of cooking pots, jugs and plates, and a "wine thief"—a ceramic device for drawing water or wine from an amphora.

Eventually there proved to be eleven iron anchors in the wreck, some of which came up in the form of featureless concretions because the iron at the core had corroded away long before. So the archaeologists cut into the hollow concretions with a jeweler's saw, filled the void with plaster, and made exact casts of nine of the anchors, so that the original shape and weight are exactly known.

There apparently were three sets of scales aboard: one was a steelyard with a counterpoise weight in the form of a hollow bronze bust of Athena weighted with lead; the other two used the balance-pan system, with weights made of bronze inlaid with silver. They seem to be the most complete set of Byzantine weights in existence.

The pottery in the galley was identified as being from the lower Black Sea and Bulgaria. That evidence, plus the find of Bosporus mussel shells and coins from Constantinople, made it pretty clear that the voyage had originated in the Turkish-straits area. Fifty-four of those coins were copper folles and sixteen were small gold pieces, all together worth seven soldi. (A soldi was about a month's pay for a blacksmith; three folles would buy a loaf of bread.) The wreck was dated by the most recent coin found, which was minted by the Emperor Heraclius, A.D. 625.

In design and construction, this ship turned out to be a transitional form between the ancient system of securing the planking together by means of closely placed mortise-and-tenon joints and the more modern one of planking over a frame of ribs. The finished ship was small, even for its day; it displaced around forty tons.

Later the University of Pennsylvania crew turned its attention to the other wrecks at Yassi Ada, and the work there will probably continue for ten more years.

Kyrenia

Andreas Carilou, sponge diver and town councilman of Kyrenia, Cyprus, found this wreck of the oldest almost-intact hull known, only about a mile from the city that now bears its name. Knowing that the wreck might be archaeologically important and thus bring honor to the city, he kept the find secret for years, waiting for the proper persons to come along. They turned out to be Michael Katzev, wife Susan, and others who had just spent the summer of 1967 excavating a Roman ship at Yassi Ada. Now, at the invitation of the government, they searched for wrecks along the coast of Cyprus.

The sponge diver took them out to a position marked by bearings on Mount Pentadaktylos and an old crusader castle. He dropped anchor and the Americans swam down. In water about thirty meters deep, they at once saw a mound, perhaps five meters on a side, bristling with amphorae. They dusted some of the sand away, took photographs, made sketches. A metal detector and proton magnetometer were used to locate metal masses beneath the sand. Based on the distinctive conical shape of the amphorae in the photos, with their straight necks and handles, Virginia Grace of the American School of Classical Studies in Athens advised them that the wreck was from the last third of the fourth century B.C.

The following year, they were back to begin excavation with an international crew of students, mechanics, photographers, and medical doctors, most of whom were trained as divers. The project bought a barge, anchored it over the site, set up a cord grid on the bottom, and began diving operations. The government of Cyprus provided space in the castle, and before long some three hundred amphorae were stowed there. Many of these had carried almonds, whose shells had been well preserved by the oxygen-excluding mud.

In the final week of that season, David Owen dug a trench that exposed the hull itself, beneath the lowest row of amphorae. Copper nails still held the planking in place against well-preserved pine ribs. They carefully covered the wood with sand for the winter to protect it against borers, and left.

Next year, the work resumed; the finds eventually included twenty-nine carved stone blocks to be used for grinding grain, lead brailing rings for reefing sail, four sets of spoons and dinnerware, and five badly corroded bronze coins from the reign of Demetrius Poliorcetes. The main thing brought up was five tons of waterlogged wood, fragments of which were carbon-dated at 389 B.C.

plus or minus forty-four years (the date the timber was cut). The almonds of the cargo gave carbon dates of 288 B.C. plus or minus sixty-two years, supporting the opinion that the ship was as much as eighty years old when it sank.

The outer hull of the Kyrenia ship was sheeted with lead held in place with copper tacks to keep out marine borers. There was no trace of a mast, and the brail rings were found all together, suggesting that the sail had been lowered and stowed when she sank.

The plan, now well underway, is to soak the wood in polyethylene glycol to replace some of its missing fibers. Eventually the ship will be reconstructed, using as many of the original planks as possible. Then it will go on public view at the crusader castle.

A mystery remains about why this ship sank. It was not heavily loaded and did not hit a reef; there is no evidence of fire or violence. Perhaps it was taking water rapidly and the crew abandoned ship (no personal possessions were found). Like the Mahdia wreck, this one bears similarities to those we will find in deep water. It sank and has remained unmolested; the mud cover saved the hull and some of the perishables.

Isola Lunga

Although thousands of early warships were sunk in wars and storms, only in the past few years has an identifiable hulk been found. In 1970 a team of archaeological explorers under Honor Frost discovered a veritable graveyard of ships along the northern coast of Isola Lunga, off the western tip of Sicily. This is an area where one would guess there would be many wrecks, since the historian Polybius reported it to have been the site of several sea battles between Rome and Carthage.

In 1971–72 a dozen diver-archaeologists began the excavation of a promising wreck exposed by a dredging operation. This had caused a shift in the bottom material that revealed a sternpost timber some two meters long projecting up through the sand. The excavators then followed the keel forward, exposing some ten meters of hull including twenty-six ribs of alternating frames and floor timbers. The water depth is only two and a half meters, and Frost and her divers proceeded cautiously, carefully mapping the position of each piece before moving it or digging deeper.

This ship was between twenty-five and thirty meters long and so was somewhat shorter than a trireme, but enough wood is left to insure that the shape can be worked out in detail.

There is no sign of any cargo, but there are parts of amphorae and two large piles of quartzite ballast stone probably from North Africa, which suggests the ship was used on long voyages. It is to be hoped that other pieces under the sand will turn out to be rowers' benches and decking.

Carbon-14 dating indicated the wood was cut in the third century B.C., at the time of the Punic Wars, although it is not yet absolutely certain that this was a warship, nor is there any clear indication as to which side it fought for. Some of the timbers recovered are marked with painted signs in the Punic alphabet and incised guidelines. These are probably shipfitter's marks; it has been suggested that they were used by the Romans in a prefabrication yard where ships were being mass-produced on an assembly line. Unfortunately most of the dozens of marks are in water color, which fades immediately when exposed to light and can be recovered only by ultraviolet photography. The divers got a good look at them when the timbers were first cleared, but with sand suspended in the water they could not be adequately photographed before they faded.

It may be possible to decide where this ship was built, because the timbers are so well preserved. They retain their original color and can readily be identified as maple, oak, and pine. Under the ballast stones, the original dunnage (leaves and branches used to protect the wood of the hull from the stone ballast) was also in excellent condition. The various plants identified included beech, oak, maple, cedar, myrtle, and olive. Since all these grow in Lebanon today, it is quite possible that the ship came from Phoenicia. Ms. Frost found twigs, wood chips, nutshells, and leaves in the keel cavity—and some of the leaves were still green. There was also a length of rope, very well preserved and looking much like modern rope, made of esparto grass.

The wreck fragments found are in remarkably good condition, especially considering the shallowness of the water. The appearance of the planking, the rope, and the leaves is such that it could be mistaken for a wreck two years old instead of twenty-two hundred. Somehow, oxidation and biodegradation were prevented, although there is no dark sulphide deposit, as is common in reducing environments. This wreck may hold a valuable chemical secret relating to wood survival.

Honor Frost's final step will be to get the planks and timbers ashore, put the wood into fresh-water tanks for three years to soak the salt out, and eventually preserve it in ethylene glycol.

A little deeper

In the early 1960s, local sponge draggers working out of Bodrum, Turkey, retrieved a bronze statue of a Negro boy from three hundred feet of water, and shortly afterward a statue of the Roman goddess of fortune was recovered in the same area. Not far away to the southeast, near Marmaris, a statue of Demeter, Greek goddess of agriculture, had been picked up about 1950.

Dr. George Bass, while directing the diving excavation of the wrecks at Yassi Ada, learned of the nearby finds and was eager to see if their source could be located. The area to be searched was several square miles in extent, because the draggers pull their nets for miles before retrieving them; so there is no way to tell whether an object found in the net was picked up at the beginning or near the end of the trawl.

Dr. Bass first made a brief search with underwater television, but no wrecks were found, so he decided to enlist the help of the Marine Physical Laboratory of the Scripps Institution of Oceanography. The following is taken from the account, by Maurice McGehee, Bruce Luyendyk, and Dwight Boegeman, of the first use of side-looking sonar to find an ancient wreck.

"The sonar had to be completely self-contained and portable enough to be flown to Izmir, trucked to Bodrum and installed in a small Turkish fishing boat."

The boat used was the sixty-five-foot-long *Kardeshler*. It was "less than ideal for this work as it had a minimum speed of three knots and a very destructive vibration when underway." They first searched the area where the Demeter had been found, knowing only that the sponger had dragged its net parallel to the coast about a mile offshore when it brought up the statue. In order to be sure that the dragger's path was covered, they systematically searched from the coast outward. Eventually the area yielded about fifteen targets of various sizes, but these were not examined at the time.

The search then moved to the northern area, where two out of six days of operations yielded useful data. One problem was that of deciding if an indicated target was man-made or of geological origin. The criterion used was that if a given target was associated with several others of various sizes in close proximity and if its height above the bottom was large, it would be considered geological. A target was "probable" if it was relatively isolated and had a low profile.

Eventually a prime "probable" target was selected for the sixteen-foot-long submarine *Asherah* to dive on. The searchers hoped it would be the wreck from which the statue of the Negro boy had been recovered. Guided by transit operators ashore and a target confirmation by the side-looking sonar, the *Kardeshler* dropped a buoy at the target location where the water depth was two hundred and eighty feet. The submarine descended, landing directly on top of a large shipwreck, and photographed many amphorae and some unidentified debris, which were later classified as Roman. No statuary was seen and no further work was done.

This find was deeper than divers could go, and apparently the sub was not a very effective or practical tool for archaeology under such conditions. However, this test proved that a side-looking sonar can find old wrecks, whatever the depth, and that cameras can confirm them. As Bass and Katzev later said, "There is now every reason to believe that such ships as those that yielded the Marathon Boy in the Athens Museum and the Piombio Kouros in the Louvre will be found by similar methods in the future."

CHAPTER VII

The Survival of Organic
Material in Deep Water

The amount of wood surviving in a ship's hull is a matter of great importance to the deep searcher not only because he hopes to find well-preserved hulks, but because his searching methods depend on having a target that rises above the surrounding bottom. The height of a wreck mound is related to the survival of the wooden hull as a neat package; this may be important to the success of the exploration.

Excavations in shallow water have shown that under certain conditions the wood in an ancient ship can survive very well. Usually the best protection is created by a cover of mud, which keeps the dissolved oxygen at a minimum and prevents marine borers from reaching the wood or other soft parts. Mud offers good protection in deeper water too, and one sincerely hopes that the old wrecks there will have become quickly covered with at least a thin layer. However, a number of other factors may also be important, such as the amount of oxygen available, the kinds of borers that live in deep water, the kind of wood and its original protective covering, the currents that bring in larvae and the pressure.

Let us consider these factors, beginning with the availability of oxygen, which is probably the most important.

Oxygen availability controls whether the environment is one of oxidation or reduction, and this in turn controls what kinds of bacteria and other animal life will grow and how fast they can reproduce. In an oxidizing environment, there is free oxygen available; that is, oxygen that is not locked in a chemical compound such as H_2O but is in the form of dissolved oxygen, commonly written DO but meaning O_2. This oxygen is able to permit oxidation of all kinds, including those of the body processes of animals. Except for anaerobic bacteria, all animals must have oxygen to live, although some can survive temporarily in an anoxic environment by using oxygen stored in their bloodstream and body tissues. In all cases, metabolic rate and energy output depend on how much oxygen is available. The waste products produced ultimately decay to carbon dioxide and water.

A reducing environment is one in which no free oxygen is available for combination in new compounds and in which only anaerobic bacteria can live for any length of time. These bacteria characteristically produce H_2S (hydrogen sulphide—smelling of rotten eggs), which is perhaps the most deadly gas known. The human sense of smell can detect it at levels of two or three parts per million and it can be deadly at twelve parts per million. Persons who say they don't like the smell of H_2S are recognizing an evolutionary trait common to many animals; their ancestors survived the deadly gas because they did not like its smell either and stayed away from it. Nor do the animals of the sea like it; they prefer, and seem to be able to detect, the presence of life-giving oxygen.

At the bottom of the sea there are two specific and quite different environmental zones: one in the water just above the bottom, another within the mud. We are concerned with both, but the water is more difficult to study than the mud because it is in motion. Near the bottom of most seas there is some motion of the water. Usually it is slow, being influenced only by tides and the gradual motion of great water masses, but eventually, in a few years or decades, it is mixed with surface waters and reoxygenated. This means that usually there is some free oxygen in the water near the sea floor, perhaps one or two parts per million where it is low but generally as much as four. Rarely does the oxygen in the water go to zero.

Within the bottom muds, reducing conditions are more likely to exist, and it is possible to have completely anoxic muds beneath well-oxygenated water. The bottom muds in places where organic wastes are disposed of frequently become anoxic because the decay of the organic materials they contain uses up whatever oxygen is there and there is no mechanism for its replacement. Then the bottom is said to be eutrophied; the biological oxygen demand is so high it creates an oxygen deficiency. Even after these nutrients are exhausted, reducing conditions can continue for a long time because of the absence of circulation within the bottom. This process is slow at best, because the interstitial water must move through the very tiny channels between the particles.

This circulation within the bottom is aided by many small animals that live in or on the bottom. Fish disturb the mud by hunting in it; brittle stars and crabs crawl about on it, and clams and worms tunnel and plow beneath the surface. All these small motions are important because they introduce new water and thus oxygen into the bottom mud. These animals live off oxygen in the water above; when that water is without oxygen, life processes cease.

Now the destructive processes cannot go on. Borers cannot live or destroy wood; microbes cannot consume soft materials; all oxidation stops. Luckily there are at least two places in our region of interest where such conditions exist: the Black Sea and the basins in the Sea of Marmara. There also may be basins where reducing and oxidizing conditions have alternated and produced some layers of anoxic mud that may be more protective than ordinary muds.

There is no doubt that most organic materials, including delicate membranes and micro-organisms, large animal bodies and bones, plant fibers, and wood, will survive better and longer in a reducing environment. For example, the muds on the Black Sea bottom formed under reducing conditions have a high organic content. Under the electron microscope, very old biological structures can be seen. Dr. David Ross of the Woods Hole Oceanographic Institution examined some of the core material from seven meters below the bottom and found well-preserved "biological membranes." At an estimated sedimentation rate of ten centimeters per thousand years, these delicate structures have survived for seventy thousand years. Other Woods Hole scientists working in the Black Sea found a twig in a core that was springy and green in spite of its estimated age of over ten thousand years.

A special, man-made reducing environment may make the advantages of a blanket of mud on an old wreck more understandable. In Los Angeles Harbor, it is accepted practice to wrap old wooden pilings with sheet plastic to stop shipworms from eating the wood. If the piling is sheathed with plastic between the mud line and the water line, the animals inside soon use up the oxygen inside and die.

For the same reason, some wooden parts survive from ancient ships wrecked in shallow water. Although the surrounding water is rich in available oxygen, a blanket of sand or mud acts like the plastic sheet to prevent circulation of new water past the wooden parts. This works in two ways. First, the mud prevents borer larvae from actually touching down on the wood and starting to grow. Second, the over-all effect of the mud blanket is to produce an anaerobic environment, in which neither boring animals nor their essential bacteria can live. The result is that when a wooden ship sinks, the upper, exposed parts are soon attacked by borers and may disappear completely in about fifteen years. By contrast, the lowest parts, including the keel, bottom planking, and lower ribs, are usually quickly covered with mud and survive indefinitely.

Marine borers do a tremendous amount of damage to wood in the sea, mainly by destroying the strength of pilings used in harbor structures and by boring holes in the hulls of wooden ships. The cost of that damage each year in the United States is said to be over $250 million. Because these losses are so large, a good deal of scientific work and experimentation has been done to find out more about the nature of borers and how to protect hulls and pilings against them. There have been a long series of tests and experiments to discover which woods are most resistant, what they should be coated with for protection, and which animals cause the most damage under various conditions.

Damage in harbors is caused mainly by three major groups of marine borers: teredos, pholads, and *Limnoria*. Of these, the teredos, or shipworms, are the most rapid destroyers. When the tiny larva touches a timber piling, it clings to the surface and bores quickly into the wood, leaving only a pinhole to show its entrance place. Once inside, the borer turns to follow the grain of the wood, growing larger as it goes and leaving behind a long, lime-plated tube five to ten millimeters in diameter. The outside of a piece of wood so attacked may appear to be in good condition even though the inside is only a honeycomb of tunnels, without much strength. X-raying the wood or cutting across it reveals the damage.

The pholads, or stone borers, especially the genus *Xylophaga*, are mollusks that begin life as plankton. As with the teredos, their minute larvae drift free with the currents until they eventually settle on a suitable substrate such as a piece of wood. They penetrate it at once and then spend the rest of their lives imprisoned in a burrow of their own making which they continuously enlarge to accommodate their growth. In addition to wooden objects, these creatures normally live in mudbanks, shale, and limestone. These are the culprits that are responsible for much of the destruction of limestone statuary in shallow water.

Limnoria is a genus of crustaceans only about three millimeters long that attacks pilings below the water line by eating shallow burrows that are separated from each other by thin walls of wood. The young are hatched inside the burrows and within hours start side tunnels of their own. When moving water erodes the flimsy remanent wood partitions away, especially in the zone between high and low tide, the pilings take on the well-known hourglass shape.

In order to find out more about the resistance of various woods to borers, the Naval Research Laboratory conducted some experiments at the Panama Canal in the latter 1960s. Three locations were used: the Caribbean side, a brackish lake, and the Pacific side, with average tides of about one, zero, and thirteen feet respectively. One hundred and four wood species from Panama were used, along with nine high-resistance woods from other parts of the world, plus two woods of known low resistance (Douglas fir and southern yellow pine) for controls.

Each wood was cut to a standard size ($1.5 \times 1.5 \times 10$ inches) and exposed to the sea just below the low-tide range. The woods were inspected at intervals of seven, fourteen, thirty-eight, and ninety months (up to seven and a half years), and some of the findings were surprising. Mangrove wood, which is hard, dense, and straight-grained, and grows in salt water, had been thought by many people to be resistant to the depredations of marine borers. But after fourteen months' exposure in the Pacific, all five species of mangrove tried were heavily damaged. Resistance to teredos seemed to be related to silica content, and woods with more than half a per cent of silica survived best. The density of the wood did not seem to be an important factor.

Pine seems to have particularly low resistance to borers, and even redwood, which survives well on land because it is toxic to many insects, is not particularly good. After fourteen months in the ocean, 44 per cent of the woods were destroyed, and before the ninety months were up, 96 per cent of the woods had been heavily damaged by one or more species of borer.

The only wood that resisted attacks of all three groups of borers was *Dalbergia retusa,* a heavy, hard, very oily wood. Unfortunately, because of the irregular shape of the tree, this wood does not make good timber, but the chemical constituents (mainly the oils) have been synthetically duplicated for use as a preservative.

These experiments led to a deeper look, and in 1967–68, after a one-year stay on the bottom at 1,350 meters in the Tongue of the Ocean, Bahamas, another navy test array was retrieved. This site has been described as a model ocean. The bottom is flat, the temperature is 4.6° C, the salinity thirty-five parts per thousand, and the dissolved oxygen 5.2 parts per million.

This time, two sets of five untreated wood panels (each panel $0.6 \times 3.0 \times 12$ inches) consisting of pine, fir, cypress, oak, and redwood were tested. All panels were attacked by *Xylophaga,* with the pine being damaged most and the other woods somewhat less penetrated in the order given. The object was to determine the amount of borer activity in deep water, and the answer was that redwood, the best of the lot, had over twenty-five borer openings per square inch. Pine had as many as eighty.

Similar tests were then run by James Muraoka of the Naval Civil Engineering Laboratory at Port Hueneme, California, in the Pacific at a depth of 1,920 meters from August 1968 to February 1969, and some additional findings were made. The wood panels were about the same size as before, but this time some were treated with preservatives, some were buried in the bottom, and some were suspended well above the bottom. Natural rope fibers of cotton and manila were also tested.

When recovered, after six months on the bottom, there was a heavy slime deposit on the ropes. The fibers of the half-inch-diameter cotton rope showed considerable decay due to bacterial activity but were not damaged by the wood borers. The same size manila line was severely damaged, both by the micro-organisms and the borers, and many of the fibers were severed by deep penetration. Both lines had lost about half their strength.

The untreated wood panels, of pine, fir, ash, maple, cedar, oak, balsa, and redwood, were damaged by the boring clam *Xylophaga* depending on their position relative to the bottom. Those close to the bottom had about four hundred borers per square inch, except pine, which had nearly twice that amount. However, a piece of fir buried in the mud had no borers, and all varieties that were suspended six feet above the bottom had only one to three per square inch. Woods treated with creosote, 1 per cent tri-butylin oxide, or chromated copper arsenate had no borers.

Thus, the maximum attack by boring clams seems to come in the first meter above the mud line. This gives one a mental picture of an old wooden wreck sitting upright on the bottom being ringed and eaten in a narrow band just above the mud. When the last ribs get very thin, the upper part of the hull drops down to the mud surface and the next few feet are eaten. And so on. A time-lapse movie would show the wreck dissolving downward as though disappearing into the bottom. In reality, it drifts away as fecal dust from the borers.

In early 1971, the research submarine *Deep Quest* was examining the sea bottom off San Diego, California, at a depth of eleven hundred meters when it suddenly and accidentally came upon a navy aircraft, its aluminum surfaces shining brightly. The plane proved to be an F6F that had been lost twenty-six years before. It was later salvaged, and this afforded a good opportunity to find out what kind of sea life would attach to clean aluminum in a quarter century. Scallops averaging about thirty-eight millimeters across were the dominant form and were found all over the aircraft. Pink and orange sea anemones, some a hundred and fifty millimeters across, were attached under the wing. Calcareous tubes up to a hundred millimeters long, built by tube worms, were attached to the plastic windows. Hydroids, barnacles, brachiopods, gastropod egg cases, and a gorgonian sea whip were attached to various parts, and inside the aircraft there were spider crabs, shrimps, clams, sea urchins, and snails.

The most important find from the point of view of the ship archaeologist was the condition of a hardwood headrest in the cockpit; it had been completely riddled by that old enemy of wooden ships, the molluscan wood borer *Xylophaga*.

Dr. Ruth Turner of the Agassiz Museum at Harvard University, who is an expert on these tiny, ravenous creatures, thinks that the deepwater species of *Xylophaga* may have quite restricted ranges. She thinks that the fact that boards a few meters above the bottom are free of borers suggests that currents at that level prevent the larvae from settling. Presumably, slower currents and a concentration of larvae at or close to the bottom would permit the larvae to attach themselves to the wood. Unfortunately almost nothing is known of the behavior of the larvae or the length of their free-swimming life.

Both teredos and *Xylophaga* attacked test boards fixed at ninety meters below the surface off Fort Lauderdale, Florida, but, significantly, no teredos were found in deeper tests in that area. This probably means that teredos found in wood dredged from great depths had entered the wood before it sank. If so, some old ships actually carried down with them these seeds of their own destruction.

Dr. Turner also notes the possibility that an early heavy settlement of filamentous bryozoans may prevent the attack of shipworms by consuming the larvae of the teredos before they can settle and penetrate. Shipworm larvae may also find it necessary to have certain marine fungi present in order to make the original penetration of the wood and for continued nutrition.

Apparently none of the borers that eat wood can digest it. Only certain specialized symbiotic bacteria can break down the cellulose fibers. This means that somehow the borer larva must find not only wood but the proper bacteria to help digest it. The bacteria must have nitrogen available (presumably in the form of ammonia, NH_3) or it cannot consume the carbon. This type of chemical process for reducing cellulose goes on in the stomach of the boring clam. Since the low temperature causes a slowdown of all chemical processes in the deep, the intestines of these clams are longer than their counterparts in shallow water; this gives additional space for more bacteria to work, or perhaps it gives more time for the digestion process to proceed. Outside a borer's gut, microbes and fungi exhibit little activity at great depth.

Fresh, newly cut woods are eaten much more rapidly than well-seasoned, aged pieces, the reason being that there are more proteins and nutrients in new woods. Generally the outside cuts of a tree are consumed faster than the center wood, which is filled with lignin, or protected with resin which acts as a bacteriocide.

Observations made in the shallow but cold waters off Newfoundland by Dr. Vernon Barber of the Memorial University show that the wood in old wrecks there is usually well preserved. There seem to be relatively fewer borers (many fewer tunnels per square inch in spruce) than in tropical waters, partly because of the silt and reduced salinity but more likely because the water temperature rarely rises above 6° C. He has explored the wreck of H.M.S. *Sapphire,* sunk in action in 1696 at Bay Bulls on a silty bottom. The wood is oak, and its inner part is as sound as the day the ship was built, although the outermost centimeter is riddled with *Limnoria* borings.

After being long under water, some woods appear to become resistant to borer attack. Very old ship timbers exposed by archaeologists do not seem to be readily attacked, perhaps because the nutrients have disappeared. It is said that one group of Mediterranean marine archaeologists, on leaving a wreck for the winter season, accidentally left a hammer behind. When they returned the following year, they found the hammer handle had been extensively attacked but the wreck timbers, several thousand years old, were untouched.

It is an interesting question how the borers survive for such long periods of time without a home or food. These creatures start with an isolated piece of wood on the deep-sea floor and eat away at it until they have destroyed their own home. The adults have no place to go after they have consumed their own house, so presumably they die or go into a state of suspended animation. The tiny planktonic offspring they produce in great abundance can only drift with the slow currents, during which time metamorphosis is delayed. These larvae settle and become viable adults only when chance encounter brings them into contact with a piece of wood. No one knows how long they can survive in the planktonic form, but it may be years. Presumably in a year of very slow drifting a few of the countless thousands of offspring will find some wood and go through the cycle again to perpetuate the species. As Dr. Turner says, "Their high reproductive rate, high population density, rapid growth, early maturity, and utilization of a transient habitat classify them as opportunistic species—probably the most important species involved in decomposing woody plant material in the deep sea."

It is possible the larvae can live for hundreds of years. In that case they can afford to wait for the next piece of wood to come to them. Eventually, with the larvae or perhaps quiescent adults spread out over huge areas of sea floor, a piece of wood will fall and the cycle will start again. It may be that there are already borer larvae quietly waiting all over the sea bottom for wooden ships to fall and feed them. The slowness of life processes and metabolism in deep water thus are made to work to their advantage.

Another suggestion is that viable larvae near the sea surface become attached to sedimentary particles of dust and are carried downward by them, creating a continuing rain of incipient borers. This could explain the ubiquity of larvae without requiring very long periods of suspended animation. In any case, it is evident that chance plays a substantial part in deciding whether deep hulks will be attacked.

Sometimes scientific evidence about the ocean bottom comes in curious, unexpected ways. On October 16, 1968, the research submersible *Alvin* of the Woods Hole Oceanographic Institution sank when a cable parted as it was being lowered into the water. Three crewmen who had just boarded her barely got out the hatch and swam clear. The location was in 1,540 meters of water 135 miles from its home port of Woods Hole, Massachusetts. Later the small sub was photographed resting on the bottom by the U. S. Navy's deep-search ship *Mizar,* and the photos showed that the hatch was still open. On September 1, 1969, a year after it sank, the *Alvin* was found; another submarine attached a line, and the little sub was brought to the surface again. When it was pumped out, the crew's lunch was recovered; it consisted of two Thermos bottles filled with bouillon and a plastic box containing sandwiches and apples. From general appearance, taste, smell, consistency, and preliminary bacteriological and biochemical assays, these foods were exceedingly well preserved. But when they were moved to a refrigerator at 3° C (about the same temperature as the sea bottom), the starchy and proteinaceous materials spoiled in a few weeks.

This unexpected finding clearly was of significance, and Dr. H. W. Jannasch and some associates at Woods Hole at once began looking into the circumstances of preservation. The temperature in the *Alvin* had been nearly freezing, and the pressure was 150 atmospheres. There was no evidence of reducing conditions or any noticeable lack of dissolved oxygen in the water in either the hull or the plastic container. There seemed to be nothing that could have acted as an inadvertent preservative.

The bouillon had mixed with a little sea water when the plastic top caved in under pressure, and the sandwiches (wrapped in wax paper) were soggy, but apparently both were otherwise unchanged. When pieces of bread were streaked on sea-water agar, bacteria and molds grew profusely. In another test, some of the bread decayed in six weeks and the bologna spoiled in four weeks at 3° C (and in only five days at room temperature).

The two apples had a pickled appearance but showed no signs of decay. The soup, originally prepared from canned meat extract, was palatable, either hot or cold. In other words, the fresh-

fruit preservation equaled the best of careful storage at the surface, and the other materials survived far better than they would
have in normal refrigeration.

Why? The implications, if these circumstances are generally true
on the deep-sea bottom, are very important. Can it be that
microbial action is brought to a standstill by high pressure or
some other factor? It had generally been thought that bacteria
would be very active at depth if ample energy and nutrients were
available. But most of the actual experiments had been made
under shallow-water, near-surface conditions because of the considerable difficulties of handling cultures and making measurements under high pressure. But now an accident had exposed
many fascinating new possibilities, and new experiments were
designed to probe the mysteries.

Sample bottles containing liquid media of several types and con-
centrations were installed in racks for inoculation with sea water
from various depths. With *Alvin* rebuilt and diving again, its
mechanical arms could be used to remove sample bottles from
racks, inoculate them, and do other chores related to the experiments. Some of the racks were kept in the laboratory refrigerator
as controls; duplicate samples were suspended ten meters above
the bottom in water depths of five thousand meters for two to five
months. The experimenters labeled their test material with carbon
14 and then measured the amount of it that was converted to par-
ticulate carbon by microbial action.

The results under these controlled laboratory-like conditions
were much like the accidental ones. Bacteria at deep-sea pressure
converted only 0.15 per cent to 12.9 per cent as much as the same
bacteria at the same temperature in the laboratory control samples. Carbohydrates decomposed eighty-eight times more slowly in
the deep sea. These data support the opinion that there is a general slowdown of life processes in deep water.

Later, these same Woods Hole scientists tried again with similar
but improved equipment. *Alvin* took to a depth of 1,830 meters
sterile samples that included solid materials (paper towels, balsa,
and beechwood), inoculated them, and left them there a year. The
results were similar; the inoculants converted the materials
17–125 times faster in the lab than the exactly equivalent speci-

mens on the sea bottom. However, similar wood samples on the bottom in open, unprotected containers were attacked by marine boring mollusks in the absence of visible microbial degradation.

Dr. Jannasch and his associates have proved that "increased hydrostatic pressure may exert an effect on the cells, raising the minimal growth temperature." That is, for the microbes under pressure to grow and reproduce they require a higher temperature than 4° C. "In an environment of low temperature, an increasing pressure will eliminate growth and biochemical activity of bacterial types successively." Meaning that each kind of bacteria may have its own minimal temperature related to pressure. As the water gets deeper, microbes require higher temperatures to reproduce.

One implication of this finding is that, in the deep sea, organic materials may last a very long time. It is conceivable that ancient fruits or food products still exist at great depth.

Unfortunately most of the bottom of the deep Mediterranean (a thousand meters or more) is a relatively warm 13.5° C. This may be about the optimum temperature for psychrophilic (cold-loving) bacteria to grow in. This is the most common bacterial type in deep water, and indirect evidence suggests that they can survive very long periods of time without losing the capability of starting to grow quickly as soon as the environmental conditions become suitable. Since viable bacteria are found far removed from any food source, this could be interpreted as evidence that individuals may live a great many years.

Fungi also attack and damage undersea wood, but their action is quite different from that of the bacteria. Dr. Jan Kohlmeyer of the North Carolina Institute of Marine Sciences, writing about deepwater wood samples, noted that "wood panels exposed for 13 to 35 months at three Pacific and Atlantic locations at depths of 1,616 to 2,073 meters were attacked by cellulose-digesting fungi. Degradation was limited to the outer layers of the wood and was identical with the 'soft rot' decay caused by terrestrial, shallow water, and marine shallow-water fungi." He saw no traces of marine fungi in the seven wood samples submerged off California although all the wood surfaces were deteriorated by cellulolytic bacteria. This is attributed to the low levels of dissolved oxygen at the navy test sites (0.3 to 1.3 parts per million). It seems likely that deepwater fungi can live at higher pressures and lower temperatures than bacteria but their growth is inhibited by the low oxygen content. Somewhat surprisingly, the highest bacterial count was found in this minimum oxygen zone.

Dr. Kohlmeyer found the fungus Ascomycetes apparently growing and reproducing on a sunken driftwood branch trawled up from 3,710 meters in the Gulf of Panama, although it is possible the branch could have been carried from shallow water into the abyss by currents shortly before being found. At any rate, he concludes that "if the larvae of shipworms depend on cellulose-dissolving micro-organisms, it seems probable that any organism —bacteria or fungus—that is able to 'prepare' the wood surface enzymatically for settlement by larvae can serve the purpose."

To sum up, the evidence is not clear on whether or not large parts of wooden hulls will survive on the deep bottom of the Mediterranean. Generally, high pressure and low light levels seem to improve the chances; warm bottom water and widespread borer larvae decrease them. A mud cover that keeps out oxygen and prevents borer larvae from settling will be very helpful; a reducing environment will be best of all. We must discover the facts by searching.

CHAPTER VIII

Deepwater Search

Virtually all ancient wrecks found until the present decade were discovered accidentally by divers searching for sponges or corals in water depths rarely exceeding forty meters. But now accidental finds are not good enough; the modern searcher requires a specific strategy, a set of tactics, and the best of seagoing technology. The chances of finding a wreck on the broad, muddy plains and in the rocky gaps of the deep would be much too slim without a careful operating plan.

Our strategy will be as follows: We will search along the most heavily traveled ancient routes where the incidence of loss would be greatest. The initial searches will be in modest depths of a hundred to five hundred meters on flat, muddy bottoms outside the twelve-mile limit. Eventually the work will extend to greater depths, to rocky areas, and to co-operative ventures with local governments inside the twelve-mile limit.

The tactics will be to select an area of such size it can be searched in a reasonable length of time, establish a precise navigation system, recheck the depths shown on the charts, and test the bottom characteristics so that we have confidence that the search methods to be used will function properly. Once the search begins, it will be most efficient if it continues around the clock, with the men working four hours on, eight hours off. The searchers will note the precise position of any contacts made with possible wrecks so that the ship can return to examine these in detail later on. How much later that will be depends on the number of contacts made and the evaluation of the evidence by the scientists in the control room. Early in the search, one or two contacts may be looked at with television to determine if they are natural features, recent ships, or some other kind of anomalies. This information will guide later decisions about what kinds of objects are most likely to be the ones sought.

When the searcher does not know for certain that a target (wreck) exists, it is not necessary to search every square meter of the bottom. If a "holiday," or space between search lanes, is left, it is not as important as it would be if one were searching for a ship known to be lost in the area. Rather, the idea is to cover as much territory as possible and thus optimize the likelihood of encountering an ancient wreck. The chances are as good one place as another within the area selected.

When the best of seagoing technology is specifically applied to searching, it includes three main kinds of tools: a proper ship, a precise navigation system, and a means of detecting evidence of wrecks on the sea bottom.

Most often, the ship used for searching will be the same one used for inspection and salvage. Various kinds of small ships from twenty to forty meters in length might be used for searching, but probably the best type for all aspects of moderate-depth search, inspection, and salvage work will be a small offshore supply boat. This kind of vessel is described in the next chapter; its use is presumed here.

The equipments used for navigation and for wreck detection are of equal importance in a search system. Neither is of much value without the other. First we will consider precise navigation techniques. The searching ship must know exactly where it is at all times. "Exactly" in searching is usually taken to mean the ability to return to within fifty meters of a point previously established. This is about one ship length, and it insures that only a small amount of repeat searching must be done to find a specific small object on the bottom. Ships crossing the ocean ordinarily know their position on the earth's surface within about a mile. In searching, it is usually not necessary to know the ship's position on the globe but it is very important to know its exact location relative to a fixed point on the bottom or to an arbitrary searching grid so that any contacts made by the wreck-detection equipment can be found again.

For shallow-water, near-shore operations in daylight, a simple combination of buoys and range markers ashore, transits and radios, or sextants may be adequate. But offshore, deepwater search and recovery with an expensive ship and survey party means around-the-clock operations, often in rough weather. For this, one of several varieties of electronic systems must be employed. Sometimes shore stations several hundred miles away can be used to obtain the ship's position with an accuracy of a few hundred meters. However, in searching it is usually preferable to combine such remote position indication with a specialized local positioning scheme involving special buoys or bottom markers.

The principal long-range navigation systems are loran and omega. They are operated by governments for general navigational use, but they are not sufficiently accurate to be of much assistance to an archaeological search in the Mediterranean or Black Sea. An alternative is to establish pairs of privately operated stations on shores as near as possible to the area to be searched. Intermediate-range (over-the-horizon) systems such as Raydist, shoran, and Decca can give a ship's position more closely, but they are expensive and have certain operating problems that include a shift in the ship's apparent position as the height of the ionosphere changes at sunrise and sunset. All these navigational systems require pairs of shore stations whose distance from each other is precisely known. Then, by phase-matching radio waves and by triangulation, the ship's position at the third corner of the triangle can be worked out.

Within sight of land, a distance that is generally within about thirty miles but depends both on the height of the land and the elevation of the observer or aerial above the sea, line-of-sight electronics is preferred. Various systems such as Decca Trisponder, Cubic Autotape, and Tellurometer can be used to obtain the ship's position within a few meters. Generally, these require one to set up radio transponders at known positions ashore and to record and plot the range to each.

Beyond the line-of-sight range, an entirely local system that relates the ship's position to the sea floor directly (rather than to known points ashore) gives the most accurate and useful navigational data. One may not know the ship's exact position on the face of the earth but it is known precisely relative to the search area. This class of methods makes use of either deep, taut-moored buoys whose surface floats are marked with flags, lights, and radar transponders, or sonar transponders mounted on the buoys or on the sea floor. The buoys or transponders are placed in a triangular pattern of appropriate size, and a precise fix can be obtained over many square miles. One advantage of a local system is that no shore stations are required, so that it can be installed even if there is no communication with the governments of the nearest countries.

In the mid 1960s, my company, Ocean Science and Engineering, Inc., was engaged in searching for diamonds beneath the sea off the coast of South West Africa. That coast is very rugged, totally uninhabited, and swept by huge breakers that prevent any operations across the beach. In nearly a thousand miles of coast, there are only three harbors.

It was essential that the survey ship's position be known precisely at all times, so the following method was used. We installed radar transponders on high points at about five-mile intervals along the coast. This required a substantial surveying effort because there are no roads in this waterless, trackless section of the Namib Desert, where coastal sand dunes rise two hundred meters from the sea and jagged, wind-swept rocks look like they should be inhabited by dinosaurs. So we got about in four-wheel-drive Land-Rovers and helicopters, leapfrogging the survey stations from rock to rock and from dune to dune.

The surveyors used theodolites to turn angles between points several miles apart that could be seen through the rising heat waves only when they were marked by the flash of the sun on an aimed mirror. Distance between the points was measured by the Tellurometer, a sort of electronic tape measure. As the line of transponders marched slowly up the coast, the various shore-party units and the ship were in constant radio communication to make sure the ship was properly identifying the various transponders and that no one disappeared in the desert along the Skeleton Coast.

The radar transponders we set out were small, self-powered units that would detect the ship's radar signal and repeat it back. These showed on the ship's radarscope as very bright dots that were easily identifiable. Electronically controlled range rings on the scope were then adjusted to be just tangent to a bright dot. These had been calibrated by Alpine Geophysical Corp. so that the distance between the ship and the transponder could be read directly in meters. Since the locations of the points ashore were known precisely, fixes on pairs of transponders at two-minute intervals exactly fixed the ship's position. Successive positions gave the ship's track at specific times, and these were noted on the geophysical record. Finally the information was fed directly from the range rings to lead screws attached to plotting arms. When the arms were set up on an accurate chart of the coast, the ship's position was plotted automatically.

A variation on this scheme that can be used in deep water far at sea is to install radar transponders on the surface floats of deep-moored buoys that are set out in the search area. The taut-moored buoy for very deep water was invented by the author in 1950 as a means of instrumenting the first large thermonuclear explosions at Eniwetok Atoll. On that occasion, it was necessary to measure the air shock wave and the water waves created by the explosions well out at sea in the open Pacific. This meant the creation of a steady, unmoving platform below the effects of the trade-wind seas. My solution was to use an underwater buoy whose excess buoyancy pulled upward very hard against a slender steel wire connected to a heavy clump anchor on the sea bottom. The buoy could sway slightly but could not describe the large circles that are characteristic of surface buoys or anchored ships. The taut-moored buoy that held the sensors was about fifty meters below the surface; to it, a surface-marker float that supported recorders and instruments was attached. The latter did move about within the limits of its short tether, but still it was a far better position reference than one could get from any ordinary electronic navigation system.

Much later, during the first Mohole drilling, in a water depth of four thousand meters, I used this taut-moored buoy system to mark the drilling ship's position. Sonar transponders were mounted on the subsurface buoy and radar reflectors on the surface floats. We estimated that the ship held position within a circle of eighty meters diameter for nearly a month in spite of substantial winds, currents, and a state-five sea (ten-to-fifteen-foot waves).

A few years ago, Ocean Science and Engineering, Inc., searched for the wreck of a Boeing 727 airliner that went down in three hundred and thirty meters of water off Los Angeles. Radars at the airport had tracked the aircraft until it disappeared below the horizon, so the position of the wreck was known within a few miles. Since it was evident that the plane struck the water while moving at at least two hundred and fifty knots, we knew there would be a lot of pieces spread around, but we were not sure what sizes they would be or whether they would have buried in the soft mud bottom. The search for the main pieces would be made with a side-looking sonar, but the prime requirement was for a convenient and accurate navigation system.

The distance from the shore to the search area was about ten miles, which is a little too far for precise work with a sextant or shore-based transits, so we decided against those methods. Then we considered installing taut-moored marker buoys in the search area, but maintaining them in a much-traveled waterway would have reduced searching time. Finally, we selected the Cubic Autotape, a line-of-sight system that measures distance precisely. A pair of stations are established on shore that, in effect, reflect back radio signals from the ship. The round-trip time of the signal is reduced to distance and the results are very accurate, usually within four meters. In the course of that search, we repeatedly used the Autotape signals to return exactly to specific spots where pieces of wreckage had been found.

Another kind of deepwater navigation system utilizes sonar transponders. In the same way that radar transponders send back a radio wave, the sonar transponders respond to a triggering signal of underwater sound by sending back an enhanced signal. In this case the transponder is placed on the sea floor, where it listens for a specific frequency of underwater sound. When it hears the proper "ping," it pings back.

By measuring the travel time of the sound in water, which moves slowly compared to radio waves but can still be measured accurately, it is possible to tell the exact distance of the transponder from the ship. When two or more are set on the bottom, the ship's position relative to them can easily be calculated. There are several advantages to this kind of system. First, the accuracy is such that the ship can return to within a few meters of a previously located point. Second, once the transponders are in place, then all the distance calculations and the position plotting are done on the ship, where they are under the direct control of the expedition leader. Third, there is no chance that a distant shore station will suddenly stop transmitting or that a storm, either in the ionosphere or on the ocean, will knock out the navigation capability. If one places three such transponders in a triangle about three miles on a side, it is possible to navigate a ship precisely over an area of thirty square miles.

In deepwater search methods in which sensors are towed on the end of a long cable, the cable forms an S-shaped curve that depends on the ship's speed, the length and drag of the cable, and other factors. This means the sensors trail far behind and do not immediately follow when the ship changes course; determining the ship's position relative to the sensors can be a complicated problem. The method used by Dr. Fred Speiss, Dr. John Mudie, and their associates at the Marine Physical Laboratory of the Scripps Institution of Oceanography makes use of a triangle of transponders to keep track of the position of FISH. This deep-towed submersible instrument platform was built to search for large lost military objects at depths to five thousand meters. FISH, towed a short distance above the bottom at the end of the cable, queries each of the transponders in turn and relays the data to the ship. The ship uses a similar system to obtain the range and direction of FISH. Finally the ship fixes its own position on the face of the earth by means of a satellite navigation system. All the information, fed into a shipboard computer, constantly updates the position of FISH relative to everything else, including objects found on the bottom. This method is good for the needs it serves but is more complicated and expensive than is necessary for a moderate-depth search for an ancient ship. With this navigation method and using side-looking sonar followed by strobe photography, the pieces of five ammunition ships that had been deliberately blown up were found and photographed off the Washington coast in twenty-six hundred meters of water.

Another system for deepwater searching and bottom photography has been used with excellent results. The chief scientist on the Atlantic version is C. L. "Bucky" Buchanan of the Naval Research Laboratory, who lowers his "sled" on a cable from a ship named *Mizar*. As with FISH, the sensing instruments on this sled system include a side-looking sonar that detects lumps on the bottom, a magnetometer to sense steel wrecks, and a camera with a super strobe light that illuminates an area of bottom as much as a hundred feet in diameter. As the instruments are towed along at the end of a very long cable, their height above the bottom is adjusted by changing the speed of the ship and the length of the cable.

With this equipment, the *Mizar* system found the lost nuclear submarine *Scorpion* in over five thousand meters of water off the Azores and photographed the wreckage. Later, when the *Briggs,* an old ship loaded with poison gas, was scuttled north of the Bahamas in fifty-five hundred meters, it was photographed resting upright on the bottom amid a muddy trench it had squished out as it hit. By "flying" his cameras repeatedly back and forth, Buchanan and his associates were able to get enough photos (including some that revealed the ship's insides beneath open hatches) to make a mosaic of the ship and show that no damage to ship or cargo had occurred during the fall or the impact.

The wire-towed search systems work very well as long as they are moving. If they stop, the instruments crash into the bottom. They can find wreckage with sonar and photograph it, but they do not get "real-time" images—that is, pictures to look at during the search; after the sensors are retrieved, the photos are developed for inspection several hours later. The ship may be able to return for more-detailed photos later, but it cannot stop and look or pick up objects.

The *Alcoa Seaprobe* (a ship that will presently be discussed in detail) carries a sonar transponder that can be released on command from the instrumented pod it supports just above the sea bottom. If an object is detected that is worth marking, the transponder is released and activated. With that sonic beacon in place, it is easy for the ship to find that spot again.

Sonar transponders can be expensive, costing up to ten thousand dollars, depending on their complexity, durability, and other features. No one wants to lose them forever on the sea floor. Therefore some varieties are suspended from a float and held down by a weight. By means of a coded sonar signal, the weight can be released so that the transponder floats back to the surface for recovery. The coding is necessary so the release device is not accidentally actuated by other sonars in the area and so it surfaces only when the person who implanted it wants it back.

The above discussion should make it clear that position accuracy is one of the important factors in a search operation: the best available instrumentation should be used to keep track of the searching ship's position.

This section has specifically not dealt with other navigation schemes, that have either insufficient accuracy for our purposes, are intermittent (like the satellite systems, with a fix every ninety minutes), or are too costly and complex (like the gyroscopic-accelerometer schemes used by large submarines).

Now we come to the question of how one goes about finding ancient wrecks on the deep-sea floor. A ship that is complete, upright, and resting on top of the mud should be easier to find than one whose wood has disintegrated and which consists only of a low mound of resistant objects covered with mud. We must be ready for either.

Consider visual search methods first. It would be nice if one could look at the bottom of the sea as one would look at a snow-covered land surface from a low-flying aircraft. There we would be able to see a large area distinctly and readily pick out small mounds under the snow at a distance of, say, a kilometer. The air offers no barrier to visibility and the human eye is good at detecting small differences in the light reflectivity of various slopes. Unfortunately, sea water is a considerable barrier to light transmission; good visibility even in clear, brightly lighted water would rarely exceed sixty meters.

These penalties on light are at least minimized at the bottom of the deep Mediterranean. First, it is known for its extremely clear water, which rivals the mid-ocean in having very small amounts of suspended particles to scatter light and reduce visibility. Second, sea water near the bottom at great depth is generally the clearest of all. This has often been reported, but the cause is not known for certain. Possibly, salt water, an electrolyte, moving in the earth's magnetic field, generates electric currents and the small dust particles near the bottom are either attracted or repelled by the bottom, depending on their polarity.

"Looking" means using the human eye (sometimes whimsically noted on instrument lists as the Mark I Eyeball), television, or photographic cameras. Putting a human eye at the sea's bottom unfortunately requires that all the rest of the human body be there too, with all that that entails in the way of supporting equipment. The aircraft is replaced by a glamorous-sounding submarine. This is a possible but difficult and expensive way to search a large area systematically. Part of the problem is that looking at the bottom from a submarine is not at all like looking at the land from a low airplane. The light levels are low, the colors are all similar browns, the bottom appears to slope upward in all directions, and after an hour or so it is very difficult to concentrate. The sameness produces boredom and the mind wanders; after a while, it becomes almost exciting to see the submarine's own marks in the mud of the bottom. A sustained alert search is difficult, and for a project that may require months of searching, preferably night and day, direct visual inspection of the bottom from a submarine seems to be out of the question. What one gains by using the Mark I Eyeball is maximum definition, color (such as it is), and no electronic complications. These are more than offset by the difficulties of keeping a submersible operating. The vastness of the sea bottom and the small area being observed at any moment gives a low search rate.

Looking with photographic cameras is part of a search method used with some success by the U. S. Navy. The system is to tow the camera and its strobe lights along on the end of a wire, taking photos as fast as the film can be advanced to the next frame and the strobe condensers recharged. The height of the camera above the bottom is adjusted by changing the speed of the ship and the length of the wire, in accordance with information from an echo sounder at the camera. Experience combined with trial and error is used to determine the amount of light required and the height from which the bottom can best be seen.

Professor Harold Edgerton, inventor of many high-speed photographic techniques, has long been expert in deepwater photography. His cameras and lights are automatic, set to take pictures at predetermined intervals; they are mounted in a rugged frame and lowered on the steel wire of the ship's main winch (not a conducting cable). The camera is maintained at the proper height above the bottom by means of a pinger attached to its frame which sends out a series of pings that are recorded on the ship's echo sounder. Both the direct signal and the bottom reflection of it make dark lines, and the distance between the lines represents the distance of the camera above the bottom. By letting out or taking in the wire, camera height can be adjusted.

The advantage of a photographic system is that the instantaneous light from a strobe is much greater than can be sustained by a continuing light source such as is required for television. With this high light level, it is possible to increase the stand-off distance of the camera above the bottom and to see a larger area of bottom in better perspective. The existence of a high-quality permanent record such as a photograph is also valuable, although, in "shooting blind," a hundred times more pictures are taken than can be used in order to insure that the proper areas are covered. Of course, photo prints are made of only a few frames, after the searchers have scanned the long rolls of negatives and marked the ones that are useful.

Television cameras are a more direct way to look at the bottom. These have been in development since 1950, when the British Navy first obtained television pictures of the submarine *Affray* on the sea bottom. In the past few years, improvements have been coming thick and fast, but for much of the past twenty-five years the main problems were how to transmit signals up a long line without substantial loss in quality and how to reduce the lighting requirements.

Television cameras with a definition of six hundred resolution lines (relative to about two hundred and fifty lines on a U.S. home set) and operating at light levels of less than one foot-candle have become inexpensive and are readily packaged for underwater use to several thousand meters. As with photographic cameras, one problem is that light refraction through a glass face plate into sea water has the same effect as increasing the focal length of the lens. Therefore, it is necessary to use a wide-angle lens to look at the bottom or to see a large area from a short stand-off. In sea water, objects seem to be enlarged by about one third relative to the way they would look in air. However, wide-angle lenses and appropriately curved face plates can give a viewing angle of up to about 60° with acceptable aberration.

Lighting the bottom is a problem. Muds are generally dark-colored and have low reflectivity, so they absorb most of the light that reaches them. Since the water absorbs much of the light before it reaches the bottom—and reduces the reflected light even more as it travels back to the camera—one must use far higher levels of light under water than are ordinarily used in air. More-over, if there are dust particles in the water, these tend to scatter the light and reflect it back into the camera, making them look like bright specks and blocking out the darker and more distant bottom that is of prime interest.

There are ways to overcome these problems. First, it is inefficient to use ordinary white light, because it is easily absorbed by sea water and is only about 20 per cent as efficient as it is in air. The red end of its spectrum will be lost at once. Rather, one looks for specific wave lengths that are optimal for light transmission in sea water; the best are in the blue-green part of the spectrum. Much experimentation has shown that an emerald-green thallium-iodide-vapor light of 5350 angstrom units emits light at the wave length most readily transmitted by sea water. When these lights are used with a camera such as the Jaymar that is peaked to receive their frequency, the television sees much better than a diver.

11. The TVSS (Television Search and Salvage), with W. Bascom, J. Mardesich, and H. Stubbs, who built it for Seafinders, Inc. The grab is activated by hydraulic cylinders in view of the television camera above. This one was designed for recovering bronze cannon and silver treasure from depths to fifteen hundred feet. (*Seafinders, Inc.*)

12. The TVSS controls consist mainly of simple toggle switches that are operated by a man watching the dual monitors. (*Seafinders, Inc.*)

13. *Alcoa Seaprobe* at sea. This is the world's largest aluminum ship and one of the most advanced research ships afloat. It carries fifteen thousand feet of pipe and is capable of retrieving objects weighing two hundred tons from that depth. (*Alcoa Marine, Inc.*)

14. Willard Bascom inspecting the special aluminum construction of the *Alcoa Seaprobe* at Petersen Shipbuilding Company, Sturgeon Bay, Wisconsin. (*Petersen Shipbuilding Co.*)

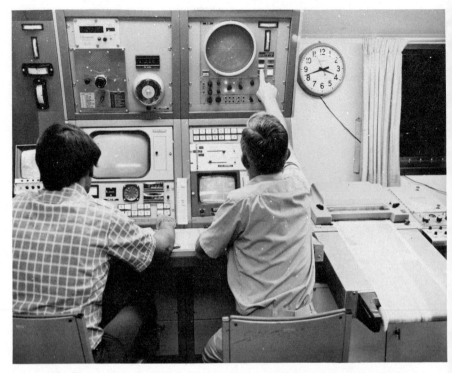

15. Captain Ian (Scotty) Crichton (right) at the search controls of *Alcoa Seaprobe*. The side-looking sonar record is at his right, the pod-position indicator is above his head, and the television monitor is before him. (*Alcoa Marine, Inc.*)

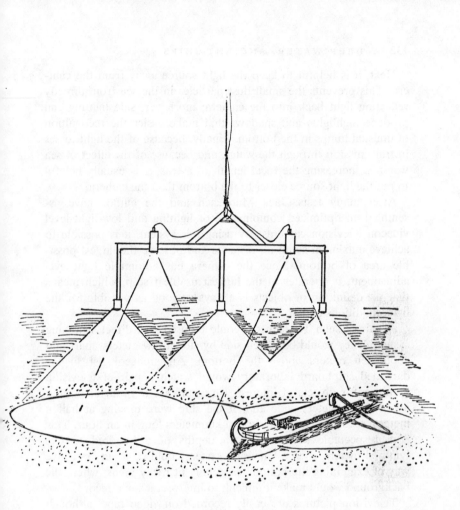

Figure 11. **Searching with Low-light-level Television**

This schematic drawing indicates that in the deep Mediterranean, where the water is very clear, it is possible to observe the sea bottom directly. A pair of low-light-level television cameras with wide-angle lenses peaked in the blue-green part of the spectrum could see a large area lighted by thallium-iodide lamps. This should be very useful in rocky areas, where the sonar record is confusing.

Next, it is helpful to keep the light source away from the camera. This prevents the small dust particles in the sea from directly reflecting light back into the camera; moreover, side lighting can produce highlights and shadows that make easier the recognition of unusual lumps in the bottom. Finally, because of the light losses in transmission through the water, and because of the effect of sea water in increasing the focal length of a lens, it is usually helpful to put the light source closer to the bottom than the camera.

After many tests, Jack Mardesich and the author have assembled an optimized combination of lighting and low-light-level videocon television cameras. By using this system, it is possible to achieve maximum stand-off distance and observe the largest possible area of bottom. Since the camera has automatic light-level adjustment, it operates at the highest usable f stop, which means that the definition of objects is always as good as possible for the light conditions extant.

A pair of such TV cameras could be used in a direct searching system. They would be towed side by side a few meters apart and about ten meters above the bottom. An archaeologist in the darkened shipboard laboratory would watch a pair of television monitors for objects of interest. He would see a swath of bottom about thirty meters wide and, if the ship were moving at half a meter a second, a strip nearly two kilometers long in an hour. This is a respectable search rate. In depths of a hundred to five hundred meters, such a television system could be a very effective way of examining the bottom, especially in rocky areas, where the background would make it difficult to interpret a sonic record.

Television pictures are easily recorded on video tape, although there may be some slight degradation of signal from the picture originally observed. The advantage of recording everything on video tape is that no information is lost if the archaeologist's attention is diverted, and, of course, anything of interest can be replayed as often as desired. Conversely, if nothing of interest is encountered the tape can be reused. The monitor presentation can be photographed by a Polaroid or other camera for a more convenient record of specific scenes. The archaeologist can also use a microphone to record orally on the video tape the ship's position and any comments he may have.

Most searching in the sea is done by ranging with underwater sound. Active sonar systems use a transducer to send out a pulse, or "ping," of sound at a specific frequency. Then the same transducer listens for the reflection of that ping after it has bounced off the bottom, a school of fish, or a submarine. The time between outgoing and returning pings is graphically recorded so that the range or depth is immediately evident. There are many varieties of sonar, each used for specific purposes, with frequencies ranging from about three cycles per second (three hertz) to two hundred thousand cycles per second (two hundred kilohertz). The low frequencies have longer wave lengths, require more energy, and travel much farther in the sea with less attenuation. For frequencies higher than about thirty kilohertz, the opposite is true.

A ship's echo sounder is the simplest form of sonar. A transducer on the ship's bottom sends downward a ping of sound which is reflected back by the bottom. Dark lines representing the outgoing and returning signals are presented on a graphic recorder. The recorder mechanism is such that it multiplies the elapsed time in seconds by the speed of sound in water (1,480 meters per second) and divides by two. The record thus shows the depth of the water or the range to the first object encountered by the sound.

Deepwater echo sounders usually operate at frequencies of ten or twelve kilohertz, projecting sound downward through a conical volume of water whose apex angle is about 45°. Shallow-water echo sounders use higher frequencies but less power; their signal will not reflect from any great depth because of the attenuation of sea water, but they measure depth more accurately in shallow water because the wave length is smaller and the cone, or beam, of the outgoing signal is only a few degrees.

For geological studies it is sometimes useful to probe beneath the sea bottom and determine the depth to various subbottom layers caused by changes in the type of sediment. Sonars used for this purpose have low frequencies, of around 3.5 kilohertz, and they can penetrate dozens of meters into the sea muds, being reflected by any object there (larger than about five meters across) that has different properties from the material around it.

Using one kind of low-frequency equipment, called a "boomer,"

Professor Edgerton and Peter Throckmorton looked beneath the bottoms of a number of Greek harbors and got reflections that apparently were of old ships. Of the fifteen such indications they got at Methone, the three they checked with diver-dug trenches all turned out to be old ship hulls buried in the mud. Bottom-penetrating sonar can be a useful tool in certain kinds of archaeological work, but it "sees" only a small area directly under the transducer, which itself must be near the bottom. A search with such equipment would be logical only if there were other indications of a wreck in the area. For example, a known wreck lost beneath mud after a storm, or a specific reference in ancient literature to a sinking in a restricted waterway.

The high-frequency sonars have more application to the work proposed here, because their narrow, searchlight-like beam can be aimed and their short wave lengths give better definition.

Searchlight sonars that can be trained on schools of fish or underwater structures have been in use by fishermen and navy salvage men for many years. The problem is that a point of sound does not generate a picture, as does light, but gives only the range to the first object encountered. Although the searchlight can be slowly scanned back and forth to build up a picture, this is a slow process. During this time, the ship on which it is mounted has also moved, so that the sonic picture becomes badly warped. A searcher looking for hulks and humps needs a better, more three-dimensional picture of the sea floor.

The side-looking sonar gives such a picture. It uses a horizontally elongated transducer to produce not a pencil-like beam but a fan-shaped pattern of sound that is very narrow in one dimension and very wide in the other. At intervals of about one second, pulses of sound are projected and the echoes received. These reflections from the sea floor are recorded as a thin tan line whose density varies with the strength of the echo.

If a pair of these tranducers are placed back to back and towed near the sea bottom, the double fan of sound covers a pathway several hundred meters wide perpendicular to the ship's track. After each pulse, the reflection of the nearby bottom returns first, followed by those of points successively farther away. Returning echoes from a plain mud bottom produce an even-colored tan on the graphic record. However, if some hard object such as a hull rises above the bottom, it reflects the sound better than the mud, so the record shows a concentrated, dark line; beyond that, there is a white "shadow" in the "lee" of the hull, representing a time when no sound was being reflected from the bottom; finally the normal tan of undisturbed mud resumes.

A picture of the bottom develops as a succession of lines accumulates on the record. When several adjacent sound beams encounter an unusual object rising above the bottom and changing the normal reflectivity, it will be evident to the watcher although sometimes the variations in chart density are very small. As with other technical specialties, the successful use of side-looking sonar depends to a considerable extent on the interest and talent of the operator.

Modern side-looking sonars are a very effective way of searching large areas of the sea floor that are flat and muddy. These instruments generally operate at frequencies of from a hundred to a hundred and eighty kilohertz, which means that they project sound in a wafer-thin beam about one half degree wide. At high power levels, these transducers can get reflections back from the bottom three hundred meters and more on each side of the towing ship's path. The idea is to tow the transducer at some optimum height above the bottom so that the angles at which the sonar beam strikes the sea floor are best for searching. This is often about sixty meters, or one fifth of the maximum effective reach. The pings go out at about one-second intervals and, with a ship speed of around one half meter per second, the bottom areas touched by successive sonar pings overlap slightly.

Using the above figures (that is, a sweep path of six hundred meters and a ship speed of half a meter per second), this sonar will search one square kilometer every hour. The work can be continuous, around the clock, if the persons operating the ship, plotting its successive positions, and watching the graphic recording of the echoes are relieved at frequent intervals.

One problem with this kind of sonar is that, in areas where the sea bottom is rocky and irregular, there will be a large number of shadows not caused by shipwrecks. These will be confusing, and

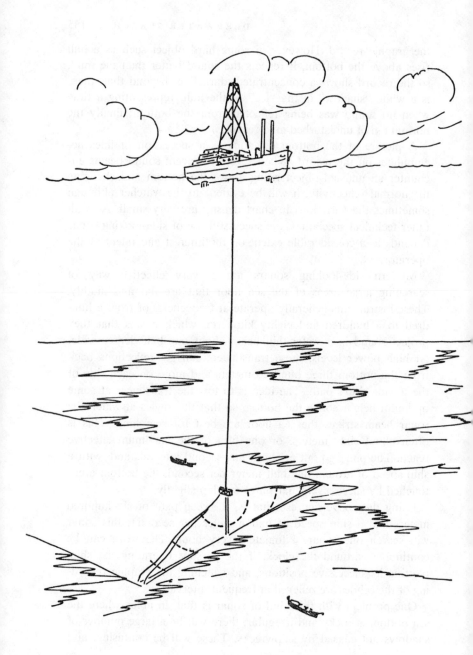

there are likely to be far too many of them to check out. Therefore one concludes that sonar is not a good search system except on a reasonably flat muddy bottom on which bumps are rare.

Some ancient wrecks may contain sufficient iron that on occasion it will be sensible to search with a magnetometer. This will be a particularly useful technique if sand or mud covers a hull known to exist from other evidence. Ancient ships probably did not have much iron aboard. One would expect nails, ship fittings, anchors, parts of war machines, and some lesser military hardware. Under salt water, most of these probably became iron oxides and then disintegrated in their first thousand years on the bottom. As the minute particles of iron from disintegrating ship parts diffuse outward through the mud and overburden, they orient themselves with the earth's magnetic field, forming a low-grade but coherent field of their own. It may be possible to detect this with a good magnetometer if the magnetic background in the area is low.

Almost certainly, any large magnetic anomalies found would be caused by more modern ships. However, it is well to be able to call on the best of modern technology if it be needed, and there is some possibility of a magnetic signature associated with an ancient shipwreck.

Searching for bronze objects buried in the sea-floor muds will be even more difficult, and one must make use of a different set of physical principles. For this work, an electronic metal locator is appropriate. These are commonly used to find small metal objects such as coins beneath a shallow cover of soil, and some varieties are already used by divers to find large iron pipes buried as much

Figure 12. **Searching with Side-looking Sonar**
    This sonar is the most efficient way to search for ship hulks on a flat sea floor. A pair of transducers mounted on an instrument pod towed below the search ship radiate narrow beams of sound perpendicular to the path of the ship. The reflected signal is recorded in such a manner that any object rising above the bottom casts a white sonic shadow on the chart.

as two meters beneath the mud in water depths to a hundred meters. The Army uses similar instruments to detect land mines, and thousands of people spend their spare time hunting with them for old coins and artifacts on beaches.

There are several varieties of metal locators that work on similar principles. Generally, two loop antennas are used, one of which transmits a predictable electromagnetic field and the other measures distortions in that field caused by a buried metallic object. The target is said to be inductively coupled; bronze decreases the inductance.

Signal strength is directly proportional to the cube of the target diameter and inversely proportional to the sixth power of the target depth. This means that the signal increases greatly as the target size increases (a statue would be much easier to find than a sword) and decreases much more greatly as the distance from the instrument increases.

Several companies manufacture undersea metal locators for use by divers, and doubtless larger versions can be designed that would be suitable for use in an array. Bronze objects the size of a chariot or ram beak or statue probably can be detected to a depth of two meters beneath the sea bottom. Smaller objects that could have been dropped at the sites of naval battles, such as swords, shields, and armor pieces, would have immediately sunk a short way into the bottom and then been covered by two thousand years' sediment. Their influence on a metal locator will not be great, but it seems possible that some such pieces could be detected and recovered.

The problem is how to utilize these detectors in an effective searching method. One detector can examine only a small volume of bottom—imagine it as having an egg-shaped field of influence with half the egg extending downward into the bottom muds. Thus, as the detector moves along the bottom, it scans a U-shaped trough that is about one meter wide and two meters deep. This is not much of a search path, but if an array of such detectors were mounted on a non-metallic sled and towed along the bottom, it might be possible to scan a pathway perhaps ten meters wide.

If this sled moves along the bottom at fifty meters per minute, then in about thirty-five hours a square kilometer could be covered. This indicates that it may be realistic to think of finding old bronze objects buried beneath the mud. Possibly the remaining cargo of the Cape Artemision wreck could be relocated by this method and more of the great bronze statues recovered. Or bronze wreckage from a number of famous battle sites might be findable.

This bronze-hunting system requires some kind of semiautomatic marker system. This might consist of small plastic buoys on monofilament lines with anchors made of sand in canvas bags, all carried on the instrumented sled. When an object is detected, the observer trips a release and a buoy is dropped to mark the exact spot where the metal was detected. The position where the buoy was released would be recorded; later, the ship would return and use other equipment to probe in the mud or blow it away and find the metallic object that caused the signal.

Unlike the other search equipment mentioned, this one has not been built or tested in the form described here. This method can undoubtedly be made to work, but the metallic objects lost in recent years may give so many spurious signals that it will not be an effective tool. No one can be sure until the "bronze hunter" is tested.

The searching and navigation methods just described do not directly tell very much about a wreck. Mainly, they reveal some anomalous characteristic of the sea floor—a hump in the bottom, an unnatural shape, an unusual magnetic or electrical signal. The next step is to examine carefully each anomaly and find out its cause. If the original navigation was carefully done, it will be possible to refind the possible sites and begin that investigation.

by manipulated tongs. The instruments generally perform these functions better than the man. The television camera can see farther and more clearly; the swimming movements are more deliberate and can continue indefinitely; the grasp is strong and steady. Only with the last is there any cause for concern. In some excavations, a certain delicacy of touch will be needed to keep from breaking some ancient object; one hopes that with practice the operator on the ship will learn the limits of his remote strength and be less destructive than many shallow-water workers have been. Some new senses have been added. Now the remote observer can see distant objects through dark and turbid water with high-frequency sounds, and he can sense beneath the bottom with magnetometers and metal finders. As the archaeologist reaches downward below diver depths, his instruments become more precise and complex. Divers and tenders are replaced by electronics technicians and mechanics. There is more of a premium on planning and less on athletic ability or endurance in cold water.

Deepwater equipment will be larger and more sophisticated, starting with the ship. The kind of ship used makes little difference to diving archaeologists, who usually live ashore; quite a small one is usually satisfactory, and it need not have any really special equipment aboard. An old fishing craft or even a barge with ordinary anchors, compressors, and winches usually is adequate. It is merely a platform above a wreck. However, the ship required for inspection and recovery work in deep water must meet more rigorous standards. For example, it must be able to refind a contact located by the search, and maintain position above it while lowering remote inspection or salvage equipment. The ship would also be suitable for extended living at sea and for riding out rough weather. If large objects are to be salvaged from deep water, a fair-sized vessel with heavy handling gear will be required.

The most appropriate kind of ship for archaeological work in depths of a hundred to five hundred meters is a small supply boat such as is used by the offshore oil industry. A forty-meter-long, ten-meter-beam version would be a proper platform for towing search equipment, lowering television for inspection, and generally doing salvage work. These boats are made of steel with vee bottoms and twin screws, powered by two main diesel engines. They usually have hydraulic plants both for powering deck equipment (driven by four-hundred-horsepower main engines) and eighty kilowatts of auxiliary electric power. There is a roomy afterdeck about eight by twenty meters, bunks for up to two dozen men, and good-quality electronics (radios, radar, echo sounder). Years of development have made these vessels easy for two men to operate. One stands watch on the bridge, where the steering and engine controls are situated; the other is an all-purpose deck hand. With a speed of twelve knots and a range of thirty days or five thousand miles, these boats are easily capable of crossing the ocean or weathering a severe storm. Thus, the small supply boat is basically a mobile platform that can lower instruments on cables and support eight to ten archaeological workers plus a crew of seven in reasonable comfort for weeks at a time.

When specially equipped with search and salvage equipment, deep-mooring gear, and an articulated hydraulic deck crane, this kind of ship would be ideal for operations in the moderate depths described here.

Having equipped ourselves with such a ship and having searched an area and precisely located a lump in the bottom that might be an ancient ship, how do we proceed to investigate that lump?

After the search sonar has detected a lump on the sea floor, the problem remains of how best to determine what object caused it. Even if an obvious wreck has been seen by the television or recorded in bottom photographs, the next step, of discovering the ship's approximate age and origin and the value of the material aboard, will still be difficult. Probably the largest sector of time in a deep search/recovery project will go into checking out the hundreds of anomalies that will be found. This work will doubtless be frustrating and technically difficult as well as time-consuming.

First it may be necessary to recheck the original contact by taking several more "looks" with the sonar. If several passes show a hump or hull that seems to be promising, it will be necessary to mark that spot exactly with a taut-line buoy and perhaps a sonar transponder. Then television cameras would be towed slowly over the contact site to take a close look in the hope that something can be seen that will indicate how to proceed. If the object causing a sonar shadow were shown to be a recent ship, the searcher could at once abandon that spot and proceed to the next. But if it were a low, mud-covered shape that could be an ancient ship worth some effort, the inspection operation would begin forthwith.

In water depths to five hundred meters, the ship would moor itself directly above the wreck site. The mooring would consist of three large buoys anchored by extra-heavy anchors in a triangle about half a mile on a side. The ship would run lines to each buoy and then precisely adjust its position until it is held tautly alongside the wreck-marker buoy, bow into the wind. It is necessary to use mooring lines that can be released quickly if a storm arises. Since much of the Turkish straits, the Aegean, the Adriatic, and the Sicilian Straits are less than five hundred meters deep, this is a feasible system for holding position over many wrecks.

The archaeological party would begin by carefully photographing or making television tapes of the hump or wreck and repeating this at frequent intervals as the investigation progresses so that there is a record of the position in which each item is first seen. The next step will be to remove the uppermost deep-sea sediments to find what caused the hump. For this operation, a "duster" can be used to gently blow the sea dust away. This device consists mainly of an electric motor mounted on a pipe tripod that drives a ducted propeller pointed directly downward. This device must of course weigh more underwater than the amount of lift it generates, and its legs must be able to resist the torque of the propeller.

The duster is a deepwater version of the "prop-wash diverter" that is used so successfully by treasure hunters in the shallow

Figure 13. **The Duster**
    The duster is a ducted propeller driven by an electric motor and mounted on a weighted tripod. The objective is to direct a stream of water downward that can gently remove sea dust from a ship mound. The mound is constantly watched with the television camera so that the archaeologists on shipboard know when to stop the dusting and move in with salvage gear.

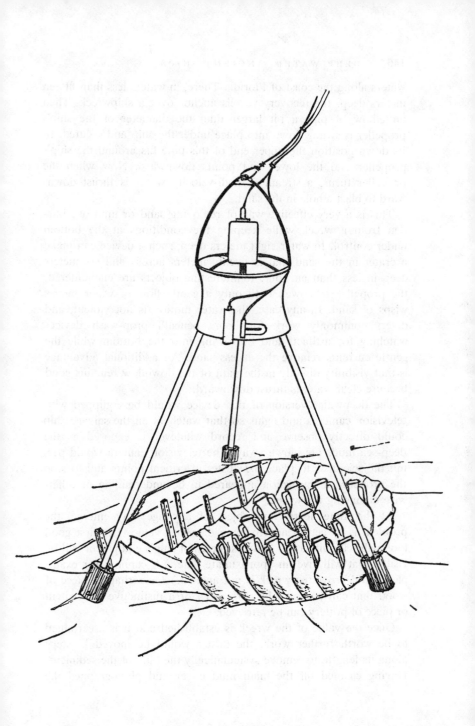

waters along the coast of Florida. There, in waters less than fifteen meters deep, the recovery vessels anchor over a shipwreck. Then an elbow of pipe a bit larger than the diameter of the ship's propeller is swung down into place under the ship and secured. In its down position the upper end of this pipe fits around the ship's propeller and the lower end points downward. Now when the propeller turns, a stream of high-velocity water is thrust downward to blast a hole in the sand.

This is a very effective way of removing sand or mud overburden from a wreck while keeping the conditions at the bottom under control. In water eight meters deep, such a device can make a crater in the sand that is twenty meters across and six meters deep in less than an hour. If interesting objects are encountered, the propeller is slowed until only a gentle flow of water moves wisps of sand. In any case, the water motion is not violent, and divers commonly work for hours beneath prop-wash devices watching for artifacts and burrowing into the bottom while the gentle currents remove the excess sand. An additional advantage is that visibility directly in the path of the downflow remains good because clear water is thrust downward.

The deepwater version of this device would be equipped with television cameras and lights so that watchers on the salvage ship could directly observe and record whatever is exposed as the deep-sea muds are blown away. The television camera would permit the scientists to place the duster at critical points and to stop the propeller if the action appeared to be undermining or otherwise damaging the wreck.

At this time nearly any object of any age may emerge; the problem is to get an approximate date and value. The first good look will tell quite a lot. Perhaps pieces of ship's equipment will be visible that will give an approximate date. (A cannon, for example, would prove the wreck is not ancient.) Or perhaps a piece of wood that can be dated by carbon 14 or a distinctive cargo item or piece of pottery can be retrieved.

Once the value of the wreck is established and it is ascertained to be worth further work, the duster would be moved in steps along its length, to remove systematically the bulk of the sediment. Having cleaned off the main mud cover and photographed the outlines, a photo mosaic of the entire ship would be made and a salvage plan established.

After the decision is made to proceed with salvage, a device would be lowered that is capable of inspecting, grasping, and recovering objects from the wreck. One of several similar schemes could be used. These are the J-Star, the TVSS, and the CURV. Each is guided by an operator at the surface who watches a television monitor and maneuvers accordingly.

The J-Star was developed by Jacobson Bros. to recover test torpedoes and other weaponry in the muddy bottom of Dabob Bay, in Washington. Basically it is a cube-shaped cage lowered on a heavy wire with a grasping device beneath. Inside the cage, mounted on pan-and-tilt gimbals, are lights, the television camera, and a small searchlight sonar transducer. It is not intended for searching but for examining an area whose diameter is about equal to the depth of the water.

The J-Star was used in the recovery of pieces of an aircraft lost off Los Angeles in 1969 (previously mentioned in the section on precise navigation). The splatter of wreckage was found in three hundred and thirty meters of water by a side-looking sonar; it was an oval-shaped area half a kilometer long, strewn with thousands of bits of aluminum.

Having located the right area, our ship, *Oceaneer,* rigged itself amid a three-point mooring as described above and lowered the J-Star cage. This device requires its own independent anchor system: Four small anchors held by light wire are run out to compass points in such a manner that the anchor cables pass through pulleys on the cage and thence vertically upward to four small "gurdy" winches on the deck of the ship. When the cage is supported just above the bottom on its main wire, a change in the length of opposite anchor lines moves it very slowly and deliberately in any direction. This gives a firm position close to the bottom from which to look about with sonar or television. This ability rigidly to hold a camera and move it very precisely is an advantage that will be immediately recognized by anyone who has lowered a free camera and watched the image on the monitor perform random gyrations.

We were able to find the main parts of the aircraft on the bottom and map them (and sometimes actually read the serial numbers). Then, on instructions from the National Transportation Safety Board, we first recovered all three engines from the bottom in a single day. The recovery tool was a single, scissor-like claw built for the occasion, which closed about the midpoint of the engine. Considering that the water was a thousand feet deep, that we had to refind and adjust the moorings to get the *Oceaneer* above the widely separated engines, and that each one was four feet in diameter, twelve feet long, and weighed five tons, that was a considerable achievement. A landmark in deepwater salvage.

A few years later, Jack Mardesich and the author built a similar but considerably improved device for salvaging cargo from old ships called the TVSS (for Television Search and Salvage). As shown on the accompanying figure, the TVSS cage, complete with its electrohydraulic system, tongs, camera, and sonar, is lowered on a steel wire from the ship's winch. Secured to this wire at intervals is the electric power, control, and information cable, which is not stored on a winch but "figure-eighted" in an open box to avoid kinks and snarls. The search director, in the ship's laboratory, watches the sonar presentation and the television monitor and instructs the winch operator which way to move the cage. When the cage is in position just above the bottom, it scans about with the sonar to determine if any hulls or humps rise above the bottom (to a distance of a hundred meters). If a likely target is detected, the TVSS anchor wires are adjusted to guide the television camera into range. The camera has a zoom lens so that any wreck discovered can be minutely inspected from many camera positions.

Figure 14. **The TVSS (Television Search and Salvage)**

In depths up to five hundred meters this kind of salvage (and local search capability) is probably the most cost-effective method in existence. Once the ship is three-point-moored above the wreck, the work can continue night and day. Various salvage tools can be used, in addition to the tongs illustrated.

The TVSS is equipped with its own self-contained hydraulic system driven by an electric motor. The hydraulic power is used to actuate the pan-and-tilt mechanism and to rotate a small "dusting" propeller beneath the cage.

Hanging underneath the cage, but attached to the camera gimbals so they rotate with it, is a set of tongs. These are held closed by a set of heavy steel springs and opened by a pair of hydraulic cylinders. This fail-safe system prevents the tongs from accidentally opening on the way to the surface. Designers must grapple with specific problems, and I was, for a time, uncertain what to require of the tongs. Finally they were arbitrarily made to grasp and retrieve a five-ton bronze cannon four meters long or the equivalent. The tongs are operated in full view of the television camera, and the small duster cleans off the object to be grasped so there is little chance of damaging it. When the open tongs are in place, the hydraulic valve is slightly opened and the springs close the tongs slowly. At any point, they can be reopened and readjusted. Screens on the bottom of the strength members prevent small objects from being lost.

The TVSS components are continually being improved, and at this writing it seems to be the most cost-effective way of doing salvage work in moderate depths.

Another kind of search/recovery device has been under development by the Naval Undersea Center for several years. With the CURV (Controlled Underwater Recovery Vehicle) system, the surface ship simply stops above the approximate spot where a contact has been made, and the neutrally buoyant CURV is lowered until it is the required height above the bottom. Then it is "flown" about under guidance of an operator at the surface by means of three propellers at right angles to each other. The original purpose of the Navy in developing this device was to recover lost (but still actively pinging) torpedoes from the sea floor, but the present design is much more versatile.

CURV III, the present operational vehicle, is an open aluminum framework that holds both active and passive sonar, television cameras, photographic cameras, lights, and an electrohydraulic system that powers a manipulator. Power is supplied from the surface, and the position of CURV relative to the ship above is followed by an acoustic locating device. The operator watches sonar and television presentations and "flies" the CURV in the desired pattern. The entire system, including the surface control console and seven thousand feet of cable, is designed to be transported by air. This means it can be flown quickly from its home base to some ship that is already in the area where its services are needed. Unfortunately these "ships of opportunity" rarely have all the qualities one would want in a good mother ship. Few have really good navigational electronics, high maneuverability, or proper deck cranes; thus, the capabilities of this system suffer when it is not used from its "home" barge.

Despite all its good qualities, CURV cannot range far or move rapidly and so is not suitable for the search of a large area. Its direct weight-lifting capacity is only two hundred pounds, and its claws and scoops are meant for relatively small objects. However, it can be used to attach lifting lines to heavy objects on the bottom if the objects can be suitably gripped with lightweight claws. When CURV recovered a NASA solar-eclipse package off the coast of Virginia from 5,850 feet of water, it set a world's record for surface-controlled recovery. CURV is clearly a valuable tool to be used in special circumstances. It might, for example, be a good way to recover antique objects from old wrecks that are found in an area where anchoring is difficult.

Two other devices that can hold a television camera steady at the bottom are available; either may well turn out to be useful at some specific wreck site. They are intended for inspection, not salvage.

The first is simply a weighted tripod two to four meters high surmounted by a pan-and-tilt unit on which is mounted a unit consisting of television lights, a camera, and perhaps a searchlight sonar. This unit is capable of looking at a circle of bottom whose area is determined by the radius of visibility. The camera can be aimed and zoomed in any direction for detailed inspection. If the tripod is repeatedly picked up and set down in a pattern, an area of overlapping circles can be searched for small objects. If the sonar detects humps beyond the limit of vision, the tripod would be moved in that direction until the object came into view. The advantage of this method is simplicity and a convenient semipermanent observation point.

Another scheme for slowly and methodically moving about on the bottom is to make the cage containing the television cameras and lights mobile. With hydraulic power available on the bottom, it is not difficult to devise a tractor-like machine that moves itself about. This system has some advantages; it can carry manipulator arms that grasp and prod and lift; it is not bothered by currents; and it maintains a rigid relationship to objects on the bottom. Its disadvantages are that it is slow, it may stir the soft sediments into suspension (thus spoiling visibility), and it has no lifting capacity except that it could attach a line from the surface to an object or place finds in a basket for lifting. On a crevassed or rocky bottom, a tracked device has obvious problems. One version of this scheme, the RUM (Remote Underwater Manipulator), was built by Dr. Victor Anderson of the Marine Physical Laboratory, who uses it for geological and oceanographic measurements.

The manipulator just referred to is a prosthetic arm that simulates a human arm and is capable of reaching out, grasping, and moving up and down or side to side. Delicate operations such as lifting precious pieces from their resting place on the bottom and setting them in a basket for a trip to the surface may be done with this simulated human arm. Such manipulators for undersea work have been designed and tested in many forms; several small submarines are so equipped. Since our plan is to keep a continuous television watch on the objects while they are being inspected and salvaged, and since hydraulic power is already available at the bottom, a manipulating arm can be added to the TVSS. It would be operated by a man at the surface who watches the arm's movements on the television monitor. Special tools for grasping amphorae, sifting the mud with a screen, or cutting snagged nets away can be built on site as required.

There are some areas of sea that must have large numbers of small artifacts buried in the muds of the bottom. These would be the personal possessions of thousands of men who died by sword and drowning, objects cast overboard or hurled at another ship in battle, and ship fittings that would survive the years even if the wood they were attached to completely disappeared. The ancient pieces would be in the strata beneath the similar objects lost in more recent centuries. In modern times seamen lose overboard such things as tools, glasses, coins, parts of instruments or engines, shoes, and knives. Certainly the ancients lost equivalent things.

The areas where one would expect many such small objects to exist would be at the sites of ancient sea battles or in open anchorages where sedimentation is not rapid. For example, the Greek-Persian battle of 489 B.C. in Salamis Straits, close to Athens, where thousands of men and many ships went down in one day in a small area, must have strewn the sea floor with weapons and armor. Certain battle areas around Sicily or off Carthage as well as the sea bottom off Syracuse or Tyre are promising. Many of these small artifact sites are in water less than two hundred meters deep. For this kind of salvage a jet rake and screen system might be a feasible way to recover small objects randomly distributed in the mud where sedimentation rates have not been over one meter per thousand years.

A jet rake is different in two ways from the previous search methods: it is not electronic, and it simultaneously salvages any objects found. In effect, it is a sieve that can be dragged through a muddy bottom to strain out buried artifacts. The jet rake is very slowly towed by a ship through a bottom that is made into a thick liquid slurry by many small but powerful jets. The trick of getting it to dig in and stay there while being moved along is solved by making it rake-shaped.

The rake frame is composed of several intersecting pipe members with jet holes along their heading edges; it is backed with a screen whose mesh openings are about two centimeters square. On top of the frame an electric pump is mounted that is capable of pumping sea water at moderate pressures into the framework of pipe beneath. The water then squirts out the jet holes, making a liquid path for the rake. Any small objects encountered are caught by the screen and eventually fall to a catchment trough along its base. The entire frame must be brought up periodically to remove whatever is there.

After the pump is started and the frame digs in, the ship can

Figure 15. **The Jet Rake**

This device is intended for screening small artifacts out of soft bottom muds. The mud is liquefied by sea water forced out of a battery of jets by a pump on top of the frame. When towed by a small ship in shallow water, this rake should screen the mud to a depth of about one and a half meters with forward progress of about one meter a minute.

tow the four-square-meter screen through mud at a rate of about one meter per minute, or half a kilometer in the calm of the day, depending on local conditions. Pulling the rake would be a good way to keep a small ship occupied in near-shore areas during poor-weather months when occasional days or parts of days are calm enough to work. With persistence, this method will bring up many fascinating small antiques.

Two other techniques that might be used in special circumstances to inspect or salvage unusual items are worth discussion. These are deep divers and small submarines. Both have received publicity that greatly exaggerates their probable usefulness for this kind of work. Neither has any substantial search capability

16. The search pod attached to the drill pipe and poised above the center well of *Alcoa Seaprobe*. The horizontal black object at the lower left of the steel frame is the transducer for the side-looking sonar. Lights, television camera, and multiplexing unit can be seen within the frame. (*H. Edgerton*)

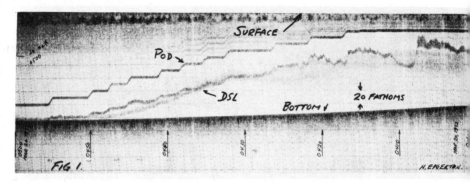

17. Sonar (echo-sounder) record of the pod being lowered at night. The pod steps downward sixty feet at a time and, since the television lights are on it, drives the deep-scattering-layer (DSL) animals down ahead of it. Water depth is 1060 feet. (*H. Edgerton*)

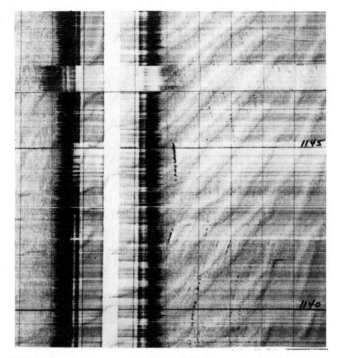

18. Side-looking-sonar record made as ship maneuvers to close on a small target to its right. The dark reflection and white shadow (center) represent a small object stretched out on the record by the slow movement of the ship. (*H. Edgerton*)

19. Willard Bascom plotting the course of the ship and the area covered as *Alcoa Seaprobe* searches for a deep galleon. Plot is carried on a special loran grid devised for the occasion. (*H. Edgerton*)

20. Willard Bascom at the search controls studies the point of light that shows the position of the pod relative to the ship. This flash photo makes the darkened control center seem well lighted. (*H. Edgerton*)

except in a very small area, and neither can navigate very well. Both are expensive.

Diving to depths below a hundred meters is dangerous, since even a slight miscalculation of decompression requirements can cause serious injury to the diver's joints or central nervous system. However, two competing systems are used by the offshore oil industry in depths of a hundred to two hundred meters. One is the bounce dive; the other is the saturation dive.

In a bounce dive, the diver goes from atmospheric pressure to the required depth in a chamber, breathing gaseous mixtures that change in accordance with depth and physiological requirements. When he reaches the bottom, he works for a few minutes (perhaps ten) and then returns to the surface in a fully pressurized chamber for slow decompression on the deck of the mother ship.

The saturation-dive system makes possible multiple dives. In it, the diver's body is saturated with inert gases while he lives in a pressure chamber on shipboard. When it is time to dive, he moves into a similarly pressurized capsule that is lowered to the bottom. Since his body is already prepared for the pressure, he can immediately go to work. He can work much longer than the bounce diver before he returns to the capsule and thence to the chamber on deck. Since he lives on the surface but at the pressure of the bottom, the procedure can be repeated for many days. Then the diver takes a slow decompression to atmospheric pressure. Divers using each of these systems have reached three hundred meters.

A variation on the saturation dive has the divers living in some form of undersea habitat. In the Conshelf 3 experiment that was conducted in the Mediterranean in September 1965, six men of the Cousteau group stayed for twenty-two days at a depth of a hundred meters. They emphasized the ability of men to do heavy work under water, such as the repair of oil wellheads. In June 1964, under the guidance of Edwin Link and Dr. Christian Lambertsen, Jon Lindbergh and Robert Stenuit stayed at a depth of about a hundred and forty meters in the Bahamas for forty-nine hours. They lived in a dwelling described as a sausage-like underwater tent, and they were lowered to it in a submersible decompression chamber. The two men spent their working time observing, photographing, and collecting marine life on the nearby bottom—much the same things an archaeologist would do on a wreck. At the end of the experiment, they returned to the chamber and were raised to the ship; their decompression time was ninety-two hours (four days).

Diving technology is steadily improving, and three-hundred-meter dives will eventually be practical. Some archaeologists will be comforted to know that a diver could be sent down to that depth on a very special job if that seemed essential. But most of the work proposed here is for far deeper water. If a man is to go down, he must be encased in a metal submersible.

Literally dozens of small submarines were built during the research-submarine boom of the 1960s, when such devices were very fashionable. Some of these are beautiful pieces of equipment, but no very important use was ever found for them and most are now laid up. They can take men to depths of a few hundred to two thousand meters to look, take pictures, and collect samples, but these returns did not justify the costs.

Of these, probably the most successful is the *Alvin*. It is operated by the Woods Hole Oceanographic Institution in a wide variety of research chores including those mentioned previously. In recent years, *Alvin* has been rebuilt and updated with a new titanium pressure sphere (good to five thousand meters) and improved electronics.

Submarines are not very effective search vehicles; when they are near the bottom, the men inside can look out with the Mark I Eyeball at a pathway perhaps as much as twenty meters wide; with television, they may see a little more. These subs do not carry large sonars, because of the power and space requirements, but some have small searchlight sonars that work very well when the sub holds still on the bottom. Maintaining a submersible at a constant course and depth is more of a problem than one might suppose. Their most serious technical problem is navigation.

It is hard enough to fix exactly a ships position at the surface of the ocean, and far below, in the world of darkness, it is very difficult. While small submarines are not exactly lost, they rarely know their position accurately (large military submarines have inertial guidance systems that are continually updated by satellite fixes). During the search for the lost H-bomb in the waters off Palomares, Spain, in 1966, the *Alvin* eventually found the missing weapon. As a member of the Naval Research Laboratory team stated it, "After *Alvin* found the bomb, this presented us with the problem of finding *Alvin*. . . ."

Since then things have improved and there are ways of keeping tabs on a small sub's location. It can be tracked by its mother ship (which must first know its own position precisely) or it can use multiple sonar transponders set on the bottom. Both have inherent problems, the latter system soon becoming complex as much effort must go into determining the position of the transponders and moving them as the search progresses.

For inspection and identification of a wreck, a small sub might be very useful. For example, it could dust off a wreck and then, after the sea dust has settled, take a close-up look and probe with an articulated arm. The sub could pick up lightweight objects and place them in baskets attached to the outside. Since the excess lifting capacity of most small subs is only a few hundred pounds, if anything substantial is to be picked up it would have to be with some kind of light claw device connected to lifting cables from the surface. This would mean the risk of fouling the lines; a large lifting attachment would be too heavy for the sub to handle.

Small submarines have two fundamental drawbacks for most operations. First, they have limited power and life-support capacity; the few men aboard rapidly tire. This means it is very difficult to sustain an operation for more than twelve hours. Second, when men's lives are at risk, everything else, including the job at hand, is subordinated to their safety. If a storm arises or even threatens while the sub is below, the men must be retrieved; if they are at the surface and the weather forecast is not good, the sub is not permitted to dive. No one wants to risk losing his men, so there are long waits for weather, meticulous checks of all equipment, and limitations on the time that can be spent below.

These decisions, as well as all the waiting and checking, all take place on the mother ship, which also does the basic navigation, maintains the living facilities, and lifts the small sub in and out of the water to keep it safe. Together, the sub, its equipment, and its support ship make a system. The considerable cost of undersea operations with a small submarine, which ranges from a thousand to ten thousand dollars per working hour at the bottom, comes from dividing the total cost of the operation by the effective working time. Considering the limitations on its capabilities in archaeological work, there are better and less expensive ways to accomplish the same objectives.

We have considered means of searching for, examining, and recovering artifacts from water depths to five hundred meters. But most of the Black Sea and much of the Mediterranean beneath the trade routes are considerably deeper. For those areas, it is necessary to devise means of doing the same tasks in water depths to five thousand meters. Now a very efficient system is required that can search large amounts of territory at minimal cost. It must have its own navigation system and the capability to hold position at a point; it must be able to dust off and inspect any promising finds; and it must be able to recover large objects. Of course, it also must offer a good, safe home at sea to archaeologists and other scientists who will be working around the clock. Table 5 lists the performance specifications for a complete deepwater search/recovery system.

Early in 1962, the author conceived the method described in the next chapter, which more than meets all those specifications.

Table 5. **Performance Specifications for a Deepwater Search/Recovery System**

Must be capable of detecting non-magnetic objects on the sea floor that rise two meters above the surroundings and whose other dimensions are as small as five meters.

Must be able to search a significant pathway (at least five hundred meters wide) at a significant speed (at least two knots).

Must be operable in five-thousand-meter maximum depth (deepest part of the Mediterranean), although it would ordinarily be used at less than half that depth.

Must know the position of the sensors within two hundred meters at all times during search operations.

Must have means for identifying objects detected without disturbing them and for having an observer directly examine the bottom from the limits of visibility.

Table 5. **Performance Specifications for a Deepwater Search/Recovery System**

Must be able to handle small or delicate objects, gently uncovering them from beneath the silt and bringing them to the surface.

Must be capable of staying at sea and operating in either its search or recovery mode for at least thirty days at a time.

Must operate in weather up to and including a state-five sea (wind 22–27 knots, waves 2.5–4.5 meters) and survive all storms.

Must be able to retrieve objects of substantial size and weight (at least $2 \times 2 \times 5$ meters and one hundred metric tons).

CHAPTER X

The *Alcoa Seaprobe*

There is now in existence a remarkable ship designed specifically for finding and recovering ancient ships in deep water: the *Alcoa Seaprobe*. This ship is a "pipe handler" built entirely of aluminum, and it incorporates in a single unit all the features required for deepwater work. It has been operating at sea for several years not only doing search and salvage jobs for the U. S. Navy, but also burying trans-Atlantic telephone cables, adjusting huge hydrophones, conducting scientific experiments, and doing a bit of archaeology.

Details of the characteristics and capabilities of the *Alcoa Seaprobe* are outlined in Table 6; it can be seen that they more than meet the performance specifications proposed. In several ways, this oceanographic work ship has no equal. It can conduct a systematic sonar search in precise parallel lanes at great depths for weeks at a time; it can stop and immediately inspect with television any objects found with the sonar; and it can raise objects of two hundred tons or ten meters diameter from deep water.

Table 6. **Alcoa Seaprobe Statistics**
U. S. Flag, U. S. Coast Guard-Inspected, and A.B.S.-Certified

Ship Characteristics

Length	243 feet	74 meters
Beam	50 feet	15.2 meters
Draft	14 feet	4.3 meters (propeller depth)
Displacement	1700 long tons	1700 metric tons
Derrick height	132 feet	40 meters (above water line)
Material, ship	5456 aluminum H 117 plate H 111 extrusions	
Material, derrick	6061-T6 aluminum tubing 5456-H321 plate	
Speed	10 knots 18 km/hr.	
Range	6600 naut. miles 11,000 km	
Endurance	45 days	
Power	Diesel-electric plant—two 800-kw generators	
Propulsion	2 Voith-Schneider cycloidal propellers	
Complement	32 crew, 18 scientists and guests	

Helicopter deck, stern ramp for small-boat launching, photo darkroom, library, hospital

Pipe-Handling Equipment—Drilling Deck
Derrick 102 feet (31 meters) high, 250-ton working capacity
15,000 feet (5,000 meters) of pipe in doubles (60-foot stands)
Pipe 4½-inch steel 80,000 psi minimum yield, internal flush
Semiautomatic pipe-handling equipment
Draw works, 600 hp DC
Semiautomatic hydraulic pipe-makeup system
Cable reel for the pod cable

Well Deck
Center well 12×36 feet (4×12 meters) surrounded by a deck 50×60 feet with 12 feet of headroom
Machine and welding shops, electronics repair

Table 6. **Alcoa Seaprobe Statistics**
U. S. Flag, U. S. Coast Guard-Inspected, and A.B.S.-Certified

Bridge and Navigation Equipment
Central controls for dynamic positioning
Gyrocompass
Loran A/C
Radio direction finder
Echo sounders
Radar
Radiotelephone

Search-and-Recovery Control Equipment
Duplicate dynamic positioning controls
Precision depth recorder
Radar repeater
Search plotting board
Search control console
   Side-looking sonar
   Pod-position indicator
   Obstacle-avoidance sonar
   Television monitor (pod)
   Television intercom (well or drilling deck)
   Video tape recorder

Pod Equipment
Side-looking sonar transducers
Obstacle-avoidance sonar transducer
Television camera and lights
Photographic camera and strobe light
Multiplexing system
Sonar transponders for release as markers

Let me discuss the main features that make this ship different from most others. These include its construction, power plant, propulsion, pipe-handling gear, instrumentation, and controls. Some unusual technical terms from the marine drilling business will be used that cannot be fully explained here, but I hope the sense of how each part is used will be understandable.

First, the *Alcoa Seaprobe* and its derrick are made entirely of marine aluminum assembled with aircraft-grade welding. This means the ship is not subject to ordinary corrosion problems and so is largely unpainted inside and out; the result is that its work spaces seem exceptionally light and clean. It floats higher in the water than a steel ship of the same size and it flexes somewhat more because of the greater elasticity of aluminum. It also happens to be the largest aluminum structure in the world.

The ship is all-electric. That is, the main power is a diesel-electric plant that generates electricity that can be used either for propulsion, pipe handling, housekeeping, or other purposes. This is unlike most ships, whose main engines directly drive the propeller. Furthermore, this power plant is situated forward of the center well, under the pipe racker, so that a minimum amount of engine noise and vibration is transmitted to the living quarters and control centers.

The propellers are unlike those of most ships. *Alcoa Seaprobe* has two cycloidal, or vertical-axis, propellers, one at each end. Each consists of a circular horizontal plate flush with the bottom of the keel, from which six rectangular blades, each about two meters long, project downward. This plate and its blades are rotated at a constant speed by an electric motor. When the ship is not underway, the blades are "feathered," which means that both the leading and trailing edges of each blade follow the same circular path as the base plate rotates. In order to give thrust to propel the ship, the angle of attack of these blades can be changed in any direction almost instantly by hydraulic rams controlled from the ship's bridge. While underway at sea, the thrust is aft, as on other ships, but *Alcoa Seaprobe* can instantly reverse direction and quickly stop, or it can propel itself sidewise, or skewed, or turn in circles about a point. This is a source of amazement to old sailors and frustration to harbor pilots who come aboard as required by law but are not sure what kind of instructions to give the helmsman. The ship often docks by coming to a position parallel to the pier where it is to tie up and then moving sidewise to make contact—a most unusual procedure. Leaving the berth, the ship moves sidewise away from the pier, after which it turns in its own length and heads out to sea.

Since *Alcoa Seaprobe* has no rudders and the propellers turn at constant speed, there is no need for the usual wheel for a helmsman or telegraph to the engine room. Instead, a steering console on the bridge is used to control the various combinations of thrust. Underway, the ship is steered automatically by a gyro pilot that can be adjusted by a small wheel.

But when it is in a searching mode or holding position above a point on the bottom, the ship is maneuvered by a "joy stick," which is something like the controls of an old-fashioned airplane. The joy stick simultaneously controls the amount and direction of thrust of both propellers. If it is moved to the left, the ship moves sidewise to the left. Whichever way the stick is moved, the ship moves, always maintaining the same heading. Another control causes it to change heading, or turn. Atop the console is a television monitor, on which the helmsman can see whatever is in the field of the television camera at the tip of the pipe, far below the ship. When the bottom is in view, this man can directly maneuver the ship relative to the bottom, even in very deep water. Experience has shown that it is possible to move the ship a meter or less in any direction and the tip of the pipe immediately follows almost as though it were rigid. This means that the man at the controls could actually keep a wreck in view and constantly adjust the thrust to hold the ship in position during excavation in spite of winds or currents that might tend to move it away. In this respect, the *Alcoa Seaprobe* is unique.

Other bridge equipment includes the ship's radios, radar, loran, echo sounder, and position-plotting facilities.

There are two other control centers on the ship, plus an unusual working area in the well deck below. Each performs a specialized function. The controls for the drilling and pipe-makeup machinery are on the open weather deck in the hands of a driller, whose "roughneck" helpers assemble pipe and perform other functions similar to those of oil-drilling teams. This is because most of the pipe-handling equipment is very similar to that used by the offshore drillers. In fact, the *Alcoa Seaprobe* is quite capable of scientific drilling and coring in deep water, as well as searching.

There is a scientific control center at the heart of the ship—a cool and quiet darkened room lined with instruments, recorders, and television monitors. When search or recovery operations are underway, the movements of the ship and the pipe are directed from here. The precise plot of the ship's movements is carried on the plotting table, and the vigil over the side-looking sonar record is kept here.

Below and just forward of the scientific control center is the well deck—a huge open room exactly at the center of the ship, beneath the derrick. In its center is a four-by-twelve-meter center well that is always open to the sea. The water surface in this well, also called the "moon pool" because of the luminous blue color of the sea there, is less than a meter below the deck. That deck is technically outside the ship, and it is treated as a weather deck; in stormy weather, the sea surges upward through the opening to temporarily flood the deck. Its pulsing in a heavy sea pumps air in and out of the room above like the breathing of a giant, although this action is mitigated by large wave baffles at each end of the well.

The special purpose of the well-deck gang is to add the sensing pod to the tip of the drill pipe and secure the main instrument cable to the outside of the pipe. Thus, this deck is manned only when the pipe is being run in or retracted.

Since *Alcoa Seaprobe*'s specialty is pipe handling, a description of the process of assembling a string of drill pipe is in order. The principal equipment used is a derrick and draw works—the latter being a large winch that winds cable in and out to raise and lower the block and tackle system from which the pipe is suspended. The ship carries about five thousand meters of high-grade steel pipe in horizontal racks. The pipe is handled in "doubles (two joints of pipe semipermanently connected), whose total length is about sixty feet, or twenty meters.

The first step in assembling the drill string for deepwater search operations is to raise a drill collar into the derrick and lower it through a hole in the deck (atavistically called the rotary table) until the lower end is opposite the well deck below. A drill collar is a heavy-walled joint of pipe (about a hundred pounds per foot) that is to the pipe as a sinker is to a fishing line. The extra weight at the bottom helps keep the pipe vertical in spite of the sidewise pressure of the water against it.

The crew in the well deck below them swings the instrumented pod out over the center well and bolts it to a special "sub" attached to the bottom of the collar. When various specialists have checked each instrument and obtained from the control room a confirmation that it is working, the temporary bridge over the center well is withdrawn and the pod is lowered. The heavy armored cable that takes power down and brings information back to the surface is then secured by special clamps to the drill collar (and subsequently to the pipe at twenty-meter intervals).

When the special drill collar is lowered, its upper, threaded end (known as a female tool joint) is gripped at the drilling-deck level by a pair of wedge-shaped devices called slips. This frees the elevator that has been supporting it to bring the next stand of pipe into position in the derrick from its horizontal storage rack. The semiautomatic pipe-racking device uses articulated hands to grasp a "stand" of pipe, lift it from its bin, and place it in a center track. Then a rolling skate on the track shoves the pipe toward the derrick and a lifter raises the leading end of the pipe so the elevator can be latched beneath its tool joint. The driller then raises the elevator, pulling the pipe into a vertical position. As the roughnecks guide the lower (male) end of the pipe stand, the driller gently lowers the elevator until the tool joints are mated. Then the threaded connections are automatically spun up by a machine and tightened to the proper torque. Then the lengthened pipe is raised enough so the slips can be removed; the string is lowered sixty feet, the slips set again, and the process repeated. In steps, the pipe and pod descend into the deep. This procedure sounds slow and clumsy to those who are accustomed to lowering instruments on a cable. However, the actual rate of lowering with an experienced team of roughnecks is about one twenty-meter stand a minute. This means a speed of a thousand meters an hour, which is acceptably fast.

On the drilling deck, there is also the huge spool of heavy armored cable that brings electronic intelligence from the sensors to the surface. This cable automatically pays out at the proper tension as the pipe is being lowered. When the pipe is set in the slips on the pipe deck, a crew in the well deck below secures this cable to the outside of the pipe, as noted.

When the pipe has been lowered to search depth, the "guide shoe" must be moved into place in the center well. This is a trumpet-shaped steel framework that opens downward beneath the ship. It surrounds the drill pipe and is exactly centered beneath the hole in the pipe deck. The object of the guide shoe is to prevent the pipe from being overstressed by sharp bending when the ship rolls or when the drag force of the moving water causes the pod to trail too far behind the ship. Without it, the pipe might kink where it goes through the drilling deck.

The pod at the bottom of the pipe string is a steel frame about 4.5 meters long and 1.2 meters wide and high that supports and protects the electronics by means of which the ship senses the bottom. The principal sensors on the pod are a pair of side-looking sonar transducers for searching, an obstacle-avoidance sonar that scans the waters ahead for wrecks or rocks into which the pod might crash, a television camera and lights for observing, and a 35-mm photographic camera with strobe light for recording details. The power and controls for all these and the information from them feed into a multiplexing circuit inside a pressure bottle, whence they are fed into the large armored cable that leads upward to the search control center.

All the information from the various instruments on the pod and around the ship comes to this center to be presented to the chief scientist. There is a duplicate of all the controls on the ship's bridge, including a wind direction and velocity meter, gyrocompass repeater, radar repeater, echo sounder (with precise depth recorder) and an excellent video intercommunication system. By these means, everything going on around the ship can be monitored and observed. Close co-ordination of all activities is essential, and often it is very useful to be able to watch operations on the drilling deck or the well deck. The principal reason for this extraordinary intercom system and other special devices is safety. For example, since it would be disastrous if the driller were to move the pipe before everyone was ready, a panel with red and green lights has been provided for the driller's benefit. The well deck, the bridge, and the scientific control center must each give a specific green-light go-ahead before the pipe is moved.

During a search, attention centers on the side-looking sonar record that is generated as the pod moves steadily along about sixty meters above the bottom. As described earlier, transducers on each side of the pod send out high-frequency sonar pings in a vertical, fan-shaped beam. Some of this sound is reflected back from the nearby bottom and recorded as a thin brown line whose density varies with the strength of the returning signal. A bump on the bottom or a ship hulk will darken the line; the sea bottom immediately beyond, where the sonar ping does not touch, gives no line at all, but a white shadow. This parallel record from two transducers, each of which sees three hundred to six hundred meters of bottom on each side of the pod, must be watched constantly for small variations in the density of the brown record and possible faint shadows. Precise time is recorded on the record at five-minute intervals, and the ship's position is noted for that moment. The same times are plotted as points on a chart as the search progresses, so the scientists always know their position and can alter course to fit any findings.

If an object is found with the sonar, the ship stops, lowers the pipe from sonar search height (sixty meters) to television viewing range of the bottom (four meters) and goes back to inspect the object.

All the while, especially if the ship is operating in substantial winds or currents, the search director keeps one wary eye on the pod-position indicator. This is another sonic device, in which a pinger mounted on the pod far below the ship sends pings that are picked up by four hydrophones mounted in a square pattern on the bottom of the ship. The difference in arrival time of the signal at each of the hydrophones is processed by a computer, and the pod's position is presented as a glowing dot on a circular plot that has the ship at its center. Since it is possible to move the ship through the water fast enough to overstress (and permanently bend) the pipe, the speed of the ship is sometimes guided by the dot of light on this instrument. When the currents in the bottom water are strong, it is possible to have the pod ahead of the ship or off to one side, a circumstance that is sometimes disconcerting to the helmsman and must be allowed for on the position plot.

When the pod is near the bottom for television inspection, the watcher sits with one finger resting on the button that fires the photographic camera. There is enough film for hundreds of photos, so any object of interest that is seen on the television monitor is photographed. This means that in addition to the video tape (which is sometimes erased) there is a convenient permanent record of objects seen.

So much for a tour of *Alcoa Seaprobe*. This beautiful, complex, and efficient tool for deepwater searching has been a long time developing.

The idea of using a drilling ship as a deepwater search and recovery vehicle came to me not long after I had resigned as director of the first deepwater drilling project (Phase 1 of the Mohole Project) for the National Academy of Sciences. My group had engineered the very successful drilling and coring of five holes in water over a thousand meters deep and then five more in water four thousand meters deep, proving that it is possible to probe the sea floor with a long, laterally unsupported drill pipe. Drilling in very deep water is not so difficult if you know how; once we showed it to be possible, it seemed easy, even to our previous critics. Our hardest problem had been to find backers who would bet we could go twenty-five times deeper than the world's record on the first try. Now I was thinking about the problem of how to re-enter a drill hole in similar depths of water for the next step, which would require us to change worn bits.

The re-entry of a hole, beneath water four kilometers deep, whose funnel entrance may be only three or four meters in diameter, seems at first to be terribly difficult. Actually, there are several ways to find the hole mouth and guide the bit into it. But as I considered the matter it occurred to me that finding a drill hole was of less value than being able to generally examine the deep-sea floor from a solid vantage point only a short distance above. Whereas the low-frequency sonar used from the surface could not see small details such as a ship hulk on the deep bottom, and the high-frequency sonar that could discriminate such a hulk could not reach the bottom, by using the long pipe and the high-frequency sonar together one would have the best of both worlds. The idea that one could hold a sonar transducer rigidly and look horizontally about the sea floor or observe the bottom by means of television without touching it and without sending men down seemed very important.

With a tool of this kind, it would be possible to search the deep-sea floor for lost submarines or aircraft, to find deep shipwrecks, to make precise bottom surveys, and to do work in deep water that required a lot of power or lifting capacity. Now nothing would be permanently lost on the ocean floor, including ancient ships.

It was on the Mohole drilling project that most of the techniques for deepwater operations that are incorporated into *Alcoa Seaprobe* were worked out. Principal among these is "dynamic positioning," a method I devised in 1960 for constantly maneuvering a ship to hold it at a fixed position relative to a buoy or other marker. In deep water, no anchor system can hold a ship close enough to a point above a hole for deepwater drilling or above a ship hulk for deep recovery.

The guide shoe was invented by Edward Horton, who also worked with Francois Lampiette on the design of the drill pipe—a more difficult problem than most people realize. Chad Ohanian contributed electronic know-how including the first sonar transponders; Robert Taggart built the first steering console with joy-stick controls; and Peter Johnson constructed taut-moored buoys for positioning. Later many of these capabilities were refined on other Ocean Science and Engineering, Inc., projects, including another dynamically positioned ship, the *Rockeater,* which drilled the diamond deposits off the coast of South West Africa.

These all came together in the deep search and recovery scheme I sought patents for in 1962 that were awarded in 1965. The next problem was to get someone to build and operate such a ship. The Navy appeared to be a logical sponsor, especially after the search for the lost nuclear submarine *Thresher* in 1964 turned out to be an expensive comedy of errors that exposed how poorly prepared the Navy was to search the deep-sea floor. The navigation and detection techniques used were hopelessly inefficient. Eventually, after months of looking, the wreck was found by geophysical techniques, photographed by towed cameras, and visited by a bathyscaphe. Very little wreakage was ever recovered. The investigating committee was composed largely of submarine officers who listened to my ideas politely and then decided the only way to search was with a deep-diving submarine. They adamantly refused to make a fair systems analysis of the most efficient method of searching that would consider all possibilities. The answer was submarines or nothing.

Then came the loss of the H-bomb in the Mediterranean, at Palomares, Spain. The water was somewhat shallower but the problems were similar, and again a huge sum of money was spent on the inefficient search methods. Eventually, after all the technical methods had failed, a local fisherman pointed out where he had seen a parachute enter the water. With that help, the bomb was found by the small submarine *Alvin* and recovered by the CURV, both of which have been described.

In the next few years, more valuable test torpedoes and special weapons lost in depths to five hundred meters went unrecovered. Finally another nuclear submarine, the *Scorpion,* went down far at sea in very deep water. This time, the Navy search ship *Mizar* was ready with a cable-towed side-looking sonar and cameras. The wreckage was satisfactorily photographed, but little was made public and apparently nothing was recovered from the bottom.

The small submarines that had been built never came close to solving the deepwater search/recovery problem. Finally, in 1967, the Aluminum Corporation of America (ALCOA) decided that a ship following my design would be an appropriate way to show off its marine alloys. Thus the *Alcoa Seaprobe* was born.

The original proposal from Ocean Science and Engineering, Inc., to ALCOA had said in part:

> This is a proposal for the construction and operation of a special ship which can search the deep sea floor and recover objects therefrom.
>
> We propose to use this ship to salvage archaeological objects from the sea floor including war and cargo ships which sank 20 to 30 centuries ago. These ships contain artifacts of inestimable artistic value and the recovery of such vessels will be a substantial contribution to archaeology and the history of civilization.

The farsighted leaders of ALCOA agreed: Fritz Close, Chairman; John Harper, President; and William Woodward, Vice-President, decided to back this project and gave it their unreserved support.

By this time, I as president of Ocean Science and Engineering, Inc., had little time for design work, and the other original members of the Mohole design team were otherwise occupied. So new men, primarily Alan Dimock, Dean Kypke, and Dick McIntyre, were assigned to the job of translating the plan and outline sketches into the specific design that would be constructed.

Although the main layout and arrangements never substantially changed from my original sketch, designing the first large ship to be built of aluminum raised many new problems. Even with the substantial know-how and assistance of ALCOA, the designers sweated over the exact design of welded aluminum joints, corners, and derrick connections. As usual in structural design, it was necessary to prevent stresses from being concentrated in such places as welded corners. In this regard, aluminum, with its much greater elasticity than steel, poses special problems.

Each piece of ship machinery, drilling machinery, and shop machinery was threshed out in design conferences. The arrangement plans for cabins and housekeeping facilities were redrawn dozens of times. A mock-up control room was created to test the arrangements of the various instruments and recorders.

Finally, a complete design was ready and a bid package prepared. We found a contractor who was expert at aluminum welding and the installation of complex machinery: Petersen Shipbuilding Company of Sturgeon Bay, Wisconsin. About the same time, three other men were added to the project: Wilbur Sherwood's job was to procure the instruments that would be installed, maintain contact with the shipyard and ALCOA, and keep the project within budget; George Scholley, who had personally built and sailed an aluminum boat, was his opposite number in ALCOA; and Worth Hobbs, an ex-navy officer, was brought in to start finding customers for the ship and spread the word about its capabilities.

Although the great aluminum ship was originally thought of as a new means of probing into ancient history, no one could afford to build so expensive a ship with a single purpose. Rather, we constructed a broadly capable deepwater work ship with power enough to lift great weights and finesse enough to do delicate scientific work at the sea bottom.

It is one thing to have a complex new tool that is inherently capable of wonderful things and quite another to be able to make it perform so it achieves its full potential. This is true of all tools, from an ax to an airplane; much skill and practice are required. So it was with the *Alcoa Seaprobe,* which combined the most complex features of a salvage ship, a drilling rig, and a scientific laboratory. During the first few months, a thousand small things caused problems: the electronics had to be "tweaked" into precise adjustment, the hydraulic valves needed to be properly set, and the pipe-handling system had to be debugged. No one was quite sure of the best way to handle an aluminum ship with cycloidal propellers. There were operational problems of attaching the cable to the pipe, rigging the pod, and putting the guide shoe into place. In theory, everything worked and the plan of action was good, but the operations were often slowed by the small foul-ups that characterize new machinery.

That the ship finally did become the precision search tool I had planned was due largely to the persistence of Operations Manager Wilbur Sherwood and Captain Ian "Scotty" Crichton. Assisted by a dedicated crew, they patiently tested and adjusted and learned how to operate the various parts of the ship so a scientist coming aboard now has only to be concerned with the immediate problems of search and recovery.

The following is a somewhat fictionalized account of a practice search with *Alcoa Seaprobe* off the coast of Florida. Actually, it composites two experimental trips as a means of explaining how search operations in the Mediterranean would be conducted. The target of this expedition was one or more wrecks in four hundred meters of water where the shrimp boats trawl deep for "royal reds" and occasionally snag a net. Some snags could be natural features but most of them are believed to be wrecked ships. On various occasions, brass cooking utensils or old Spanish olive jars have been brought up in nets torn by snags. Whether or not the particular snag we were seeking was one wreck or several depended on how carefully the fisherman had determined his boat's position while the net was "hung up." Under the circumstances, when a fishing boat is maneuvering hard to free a very expensive net, the captain can be pardoned if his fix is not precise.

In port, *Alcoa Seaprobe*'s laboratory and its scientist searchers are a bit like a stage set and its actors in the morning. They are deglamorized by flat lighting and the absence of an immediate purpose. The dozens of instrument lights that give color and character to the darkened lab when a search is underway are turned off; the air feels a little too cool. The scientists find it hard to concentrate on final plans they have already gone over a dozen times. While the fuel and water are being topped off, the last letters mailed, and phone calls made, the off-duty crew listlessly hang about the library, reduced to watching daytime television. The engineers putter with adjustments to small items, and there is an air of uncertainty.

Suddenly the lines are cast off and a crack of water appears between the ship and the pier. At that instant, the ship becomes a clear-cut organization. Once at sea, everyone knows what to do.

When the ship is underway, the pipe and drilling equipment are securely chained down so they do not become battering rams if the ship rolls hard. The center well sloshes and boils; with every mile the ship moves offshore, its water becomes bluer and clearer; sometimes a school of small fish will ride in it for a while.

In the control center, the search leader starts with a blank sheet of chart paper to prepare the precise navigational diagram that will be used to plot the ship's position as the search progresses. This chart will not show depth or shores but only two sets of intersecting lines carefully drawn a few centimeters apart. Each set represents lane distances from a loran station, for in this part of the world nearly every ship operating offshore gets his position from loran signals that emanate from Coast Guard stations along the coast. Having made a chart, the searcher checks it out by tuning in one station and reading lane distance. Then he switches to another loran station, gets another distance, and plots the intersection of the two lanes.

Today the bright-green loops on the loran scope are clear and steady. The point of intersection has an uncertainty of only about a hundred meters. When the search begins, the ship's movements will be seen as a series of dots at five-minute intervals moving back and forth across the loran grid. But *Alcoa Seaprobe*'s path is not a line but a swath; on each side of the dot, the width of the pathway swept by the sonar is also shown. So a ribbon-like pattern six hundred meters wide will result.

On the drilling deck as the ship approaches the search site, the pipe-handling team is getting ready. Luckily the sea is flat enough so that safety chains can be released. The hydraulic controls and draw works are limbered up; the jaws in the makeup tongs are inspected. Below, in the well deck, the orange-painted pod that holds the instruments is being moved into position. Technicians are putting film in the cameras, cleaning the lens plates, checking the connectors, and sending test signals through the wire to the control console.

In the galley and dining room, the stewards are setting out a meal. It may take quite a while to run the pipe, and no one wants to stop part way down to eat. So, first things first, we all begin by eating. By the time we are through, the ship has reached the point where pod lowering can start. It is night now, but on ships that work around the clock, that makes little difference.

The first drill-pipe collar is cautiously lowered to well-deck level and the pod is swung out to be attached. Its slotted side slips around the pipe and is bolted into place, leaving a stub of pipe projecting below to which recovery devices can be attached if needed. More checks are made of the instruments, and finally a fiberglass fishing pole pointing straight downward is attached beneath the pod. Then the pipe is lowered away. Now we can run pipe in earnest. The television lights can be seen glowing in the clear water beneath the ship, where they attract some curious fish; the flash of the strobe means the cameras are being checked.

Now the action shifts back to the pipe deck, where pipe doubles are picked out of the racker, propelled up the center slot, snatched up in the elevators, and spun tight to the pipe already hanging below. The armored conductor cable that runs down outside the pipe is clamped to each new stand.

With all instruments running, the search control center seems to come alive. The side-looking sonar record shows the pipe descending in a series of twenty-meter steps, and we are astonished to see the television lights driving the sea's deep-scattering layer downward. The "scatterers" are tiny, light-sensitive planktonic creatures. During the day, they live in deep water, but as night falls, they rise, trying to maintain a constant level of light. This daily vertical motion of myriads of constantly feeding plants and animals is the prime method by which nutrients are scavenged from the sea. The sonar shows that two distinct layers, presumably different kinds of plankton, are forced down at slightly different rates. This is probably the only known instance of this being so well recorded, and Professor Harold Edgerton, the underwater-sound expert aboard, will write a paper on it.

Finally the pod reaches the proper depth for searching, which is about sixty meters above the bottom, or about one fifth the effective range of the side-looking sonar. The guide shoe, which protects the pipe from excess bending, is moved down into the center of the well and its door latched shut. Now we are ready to search.

First the ship's position is checked and marked on the chart. The plan is to search due west into the Florida Current, but the wind and waves are from the east. This is no problem for *Alcoa Seaprobe,* with its omnidirectional maneuvering ability; it simply heads into the waves and moves backward. If the sea should shift around 90°, it could as well move sidewise, always keeping its bow into the waves to minimize ship motion.

We search westward for several miles, then move south about six hundred meters and run east on a parallel course. The sonar chart flows steadily out of the instrument, the thin brown lines accumulating. The man at the console watches intently for any variation that could signal a wreck. His glance flickers occasionally to the forward-looking sonar to make sure there are no large obstacles ahead of the pod and to the pod-position indicator spot, which hovers dangerously near the ring that marks maximum allowable bending. The pipe is safe, but just barely.

In a few hours, the ship settles into the search routine, and although the men in the control center change jobs, eventually they get chart watcher's fatigue. The brown lines seem to show subtle changes; faint wrinkles on the paper throw shadows that can be mistaken for something on the bottom. Should the ship be stopped to take a close look at a not-very-dark spot that is only three pings wide and casts no shadow? The object is too small to be any substantial part of a ship, but it could be a snag—perhaps all that the teredos have left. We resolve to keep looking until a bigger, darker spot appears. At five-minute intervals, a time line automatically prints on the record and the observer jots the correct time. Then he calls the bridge for a loran fix at the same minute and plots it on the chart. If time and position are carefully recorded, the ship's track can be accurately reconstructed later.

By midnight, the casual observers in the control center have gone to bed and the room is quiet except for the whir of recorders, the hum of electronics, and the rustle of the air conditioning. The searchers deliberately get up and move about to keep their blood circulating and their eyes focusing, but finally the long watch ends; two other sleepy men are routed out of bunks below to take their places and filled in on the progress of the search. Actually progress has been slow, for the ship has been dragging the long pipe against a current. It cannot speed up without excessively bending the pipe, and when it searches in the other direction, the ship is dragged along by current acting on the pipe. We move to the east faster than we move west, in spite of the winds from that direction.

Another shift passes, with only a few tiny dark spots showing on the record. The electronics technician worries that the sonar recorder may not be working properly and he must almost be forcibly restrained from making unnecessary adjustments. Once the searchers' eyes are adapted to a certain density of record, it is best to leave it alone. The search director overhears faint mumbles from the technicians that this is a poor area to search or that the fisherman's loran fix was wrong. No one ever knows for certain if a search will be successful, and it is easy to become discouraged. Only the most persistent can succeed; we continue.

But doubts arise; the very evenness of the brown sonar traces make one wonder. "There must be something down there." Suddenly we become aware that, while we were daydreaming, a big brown smudge fifty lines wide accompanied by a white shadow has accumulated on the record. We get a shot of adrenalin, and in our minds the alarm bells go off.

Finally, after an endless pause of two or three seconds, we call the bridge with only moderate excitement in our voices and say, "Stop the ship, we have a contact." The bridge gets a loran fix and the ship begins to reverse direction. Presently the dark-brown sonar smudge appears again and the ship stops; we estimate the object is about two hundred meters to the south. It seems to be large, and on this flat bottom that made the previous day's searching so dull, what could it be but a ship? The line density is not dark enough to be a reflection from a steel ship, so imaginations run wild. Wooden ships may survive here; perhaps it is a galleon! The rumor that *Seaprobe* is on a wreck runs through the ship, and off-duty men gather at another television monitor to watch.

With the target in sonar range, we cautiously lower the pipe and edge the ship toward it sidewise. Abruptly the even grayness of empty water on the television screen is replaced by the mottled bottom, which soon comes into sharp focus. It is a thrill to see the bottom slowly passing far beneath us. The surface is a calcareous mud with occasional steep-sided crab caves, some with the owner sitting on the porchlike dump he has scratched out. The crabs do not try to scurry away; probably they are blinded by our lights— the first light of any kind they have ever seen.

Now a spurt of dust arises from the bottom. The tip of the fiberglass fish pole beneath the pod has touched the bottom in warning. In the world of deep-sea television, where there are no objects of known size and there is little depth perception, this pole is a great help in keeping the pod at the proper distance above the bottom. We watch the muddy trail for a moment; then the order is passed to the driller, "Take it up a foot." The response is almost instantaneous; the pod rises and the dust stops.

Now some rocks come into view—rocks with sea growth on them and small fish trying to hide alongside. They grow into a rough pile—perhaps a ballast pile—and our blood pressures rise. The captain, who intently watches the television screen at all times when the ship is close to contact with the bottom, sees the fiberglass spacer pole bend sharply and calls to the driller, "Up another foot." "And another." "And one more." The pole tip is scratching hard among the rocks, but the small fish are not afraid and the crabs stand their ground, rearing back with claws outstretched, ready to defend their rocks. The water is brilliantly clear and the viewers can see the utmost detail in the life among the ragged rocks below. We lean toward the screen, ardently seeking some sign of the ship—an artifact, part of a snagged fish net, a rock shaped by human hands.

Then suddenly the bottom drops away and the pod is cautiously lowered a few feet to follow it down. Now, with some dismay, we see a low cliff. This is a geological feature we are examining, not a ballast pile or even an accidentally dropped load of rocks. Perhaps we are viewing for the first time a small fault in which crustal movements have thrust these rocks upward through the mud. Since there is little sediment on top of the rock, it must be fairly recent. In all directions for dozens of miles there is only flat mud, so we are also puzzled about how these rock-dwelling creatures found this unlikely home. Their larvae must drift about in huge numbers for a few to have found this rare environment, where they could survive.

For a few hours we continued to inspect the cliff and the rock pile, making television tapes of the find. The entire structure is perhaps sixty meters long and a third of that in width—remarkably close in size to a ballast pile.

One important thing we discovered was that the capability for close-up search and inspection was better than had been hoped. During the design work a considerable effort had been made to work out various ways of precisely moving the pipe tip about for a few meters in each direction, assuming the ship held its position exactly. We sketched clever kinds of jet thrusters and propellers as well as several ways of steering the pipe tip. Now we found that the ship's helmsman, at the steering controls, could simply watch the television monitor on the console that presented the bottom twelve hundred feet below and, by means of a light touch on the joy stick, jockey the ship a few feet in any desired direction or stop exactly above any point designated. At least to that depth none of the fancy pipe-tip maneuvering techniques were needed. On the test of the *Alcoa Seaprobe* just described we were disappointed not to have found an old ship but glad that the search and examination techniques worked so well. It leaves us all with great confidence that persistent looking will indeed find and recover an old, deep ship.

CHAPTER XI

Recovery and Disposition

The ultimate project in marine archaeology is the finding and raising of a complete ship. Even with time, money, and the best of equipment, this will not be easy. But it is possible, and archaeologists must push on toward that objective. Probably a number of attempts will be made with only partial success before an entire ancient ship is raised, because new techniques must be worked out for every step. However, good engineering coupled with persistent attempts eventually will succeed. This chapter will deal with ideas for raising a ship and placing it on display.

A serious search with sonar and television in a suitable area can be expected to yield a number of targets that might be recoverable ships. These will be of different sizes, types, periods, and condition, so the first task will be to inspect these in sufficient detail so that a specific wreck can be selected as a subject for total salvage. There are three main circumstances.

On a quiet mud bottom the older and perhaps more interesting hulks will be the most deeply covered and disguised by sediments. Enough of the mud cover of each suspicious mound must be removed so that the kind of wreck can be identified; enough artifacts must be recovered so that a tentative age can be assigned. Then the archaeologists must decide whether there is likely to be enough new information gained to make a full-scale salvage effort worth while. Another cargo of amphorae of known types from an ordinary sort of hull that has largely rotted away would probably not be a worth-while target. However, a rare and unusual cargo or previously unknown hull form from some little-known civilization would be worth careful excavation. It is useful to keep in mind that the main objective of all this work is to learn as much as possible about the ancient world by means of a series of excavations, not necessarily to find out everything possible about a single wreck.

Second, on rocky bottoms in passes kept clear of sediment by the currents, only the hard objects of an ancient ship's cargo will have survived. Almost certainly, borers will have destroyed all wood and soft materials so that only objects of rock or bronze or ceramics will be left, randomly strewn about. If there appears to be little significance to the details of their relative location, these should simply be photographed and gathered up. Later, an attempt can be made to reconstruct as much as possible about the time and purpose of the voyage from the evidence available.

But somewhere, probably in a reducing environment such as the Sea of Marmara deeps, searchers eventually will find a virtually complete ancient ship on the sea bottom. Its deck will be solid and the masts will be standing. Inside, the cargo will be complete as will the possessions of the crew, including their food and bedding. There may even be well-preserved bodies. Clearly this third circumstance will be worthy of a major recovery effort.

The removal of sediment with the duster, inspection with television, mapping with cameras, and salvage of small objects with the TVSS system have already been described. These methods will be a very effective means of recovering small objects in depths to about five hundred meters, where currents are low and the sea is reasonably calm. However, for objects of great weight and large size, such as a hull, or for work in deep water, the *Alcoa Seaprobe* would be the most effective tool. It is capable, when the tip of its pipe probe is properly equipped, of lifting entire hulls (or large parts of them) from deep water. First I shall discuss the use of *Alcoa Seaprobe* in salvage of small articles from deep water or in preparing a hull so that it can be raised.

After the wreck mound has been found and the sediment cover removed by a stream of water pumped downward from the pipe, the exposed wreckage is photographed as previously described. For example, let us say the searchers believe the hulk beneath them to be that of a sixth-century-B.C. merchantman. From the photos, a large-scale chart is constructed and each visible object is assigned a number. These objects must be moved gently, one at a time, into a large wire basket that will bring them to the surface for actual numbering, description, and careful storage. Sea-water holding tanks must be prepared to receive some of the articles so these can be preserved until they can be taken ashore for final treatment. Other objects will be kept in padded containers and allowed to dry out slowly. This operation will be about as follows.

The search pod that found and mapped the hulk is retracted, removed, and in its place the recovery pod is secured to the lower tip of the pipe. The new instrumentation consists principally of a large articulated arm that can reach out about ten meters from the pipe to inspect, grasp, and retrieve, much as a diver would do. A television camera and lights mounted at the tip of this arm give a close-up view as various grasping tools touch and lift objects from the bottom. The articulated arm has several handlike attachments; some of these tools are made of light and flexible wire for picking up fragile items; others are pairs of screens for grasping or butterfly-type nets for scooping; still others are stout and rigid, for clamping onto heavy stone objects. All these motions and closures are actuated by hydraulic cylinders guided from the surface by a technician who watches the television screen and moves control levers.

It is essential that there be no relative motion between the tip of the pipe and the wreck. The recovery pod must form a rigid base for the articulated arm, solid enough to take the reaction of the arm. That problem is solved by literally pinning the tip of the drill pipe to the bottom. Inside the lowest joint of pipe is a slender piston, or pin, nearly ten meters long. When the recovery pod moves into position (above and just outside the hulk), a hydraulic pulse is sent down the inside of the pipe to drive the piston down into the soft bottom alongside the hull and pin the end of the pipe in

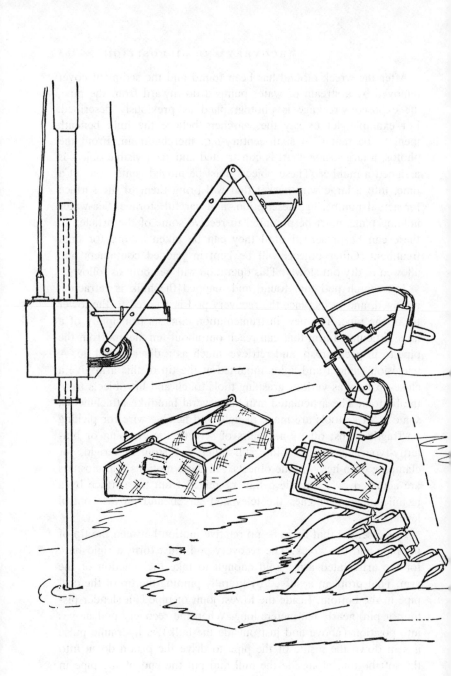

place. Now, in spite of small movements by the ship above, the recovery equipment maintains a fixed position relative to the wreck.

The recovery basket is lowered by a separate line from the ship, and it lands on the bottom near the wreck. This permits salvaged objects to be raised without retracting the pipe or removing the bottom pin. When the recovery tools have placed as many items in the basket as it can conveniently hold, they are brought to the surface for examination.

With the pipe tip pinned to the bottom alongside the wreck, the articulated arm will be able to reach a substantial part of the ship's interior. After that area is cleaned out, the pin is retracted and the pipe tip moved a few meters along the hull to a new location. After the pipe tip is pinned, the technician at the controls will begin by testing his mechanical arm, flexing it in and out, side to side, up and down. He will watch the television monitor and see the wreckage below in detail as he makes each move. Soon the hydraulic arm far below becomes an extension of his own sense of touch.

The first effort on a new wreck will be to remove the uppermost layer of artifacts and place them in the recovery basket. After consultation with the archaeologists who are hovering behind him, the technician might begin by moving his most delicate grasping tool into position to pick up a designated amphora. The opposing flexible screens of a mechanical mitten close softly but firmly about the old jar and gently dislodge it. He then retracts the arm and turns until the basket comes into view. Then, slowly and deliberately, the amphora is placed in the basket and released. The operator looks at it for a satisfied moment before returning for the second piece.

Figure 16. **Recovery Pod and Arm**
Schematic drawing of one type of light salvage gear that might be used by *Alcoa Seaprobe* in deep water. The tip of the pipe has been pinned to the bottom, and screenlike hands on the articulated arm, guided by a technician in the control room far above, are moving amphorae into a basket for recovery.

Similar moves are repeated several times until a dozen amphorae fill the basket, constituting the first load brought to the surface. As the basket is raised into the well deck, waiting archaeologists excitedly examine the old pots, looking for clues about the wreck. They will mark each one with the number agreed upon when they first saw it below on the television monitor and stow it in an appropriate place in the ship's roomy storage areas.

Item by item, each layer will be brought up; some sites, such as the galley or the captain's cabin, may be excavated as complete units. Since this work will continue on a twenty-four-hour schedule, the total salvage of small items from a wreck may take only a few days. Then perhaps that team of archaeologists, along with all the data, television tapes, photos, and artifacts, could be sent back to their home base to study the results and another team brought aboard for the next wreck.

The procedures above will be followed by the *Alcoa Seaprobe* in every wreck it excavates, shallow or deep, well preserved or not. The objective is to get the cargo and artifacts to the surface and catalogued before giving much attention to the hull itself. This will not be too different from the procedures of shallow-water excavation, unless of course the old ship is really complete and decked over. Then a different scheme will be used, but, in any case, the hull must be lightened as much as possible and studied thoroughly before an attempt is made to raise it. The strength remaining in the old hull is a matter of prime consideration.

One question often asked is whether a sinking ship loaded with cargo and ballast would fall so fast it would smash itself to pieces against the bottom. A calculation of the terminal (falling) velocity of a ballasted hundred-ton wooden sailing ship loaded with three thousand amphorae of wine shows that the ship would strike the bottom while moving at about one and a half meters per second. If the ship landed on a soft mud bottom, which is highly probable, the effect would be about the same as dropping a canoe from shoulder height onto a mud flat. There would be a substantial jolt; a few connections would crack and seams would open, but a well-built ship would hold together. We can expect such a ship to be intact structurally if the wood fibers are not much degraded.

As a sailing-ship hull sinks through the water, it will retain an approximately upright position. This is because the drag of the mast, the rigging, and the deck structures is greater than that of the hull, and so these tend to fall more slowly, trailing behind. There may be a little falling-leaf behavior, but in the main the ship will stay upright and come to rest that way on the bottom.

There is a direct proof that a large ship can land upright on the bottom without much damage. Photos were made by the Naval Research Laboratory of the poison-gas ship *Briggs* on the bottom. In 1969 this ship was deliberately scuttled in water sixteen thousand feet deep; a few months later, it was found again with sonar and photographed. The *Briggs* looked about as good on the bottom as it had on the surface—a most remarkable circumstance, considering its weight of some twelve thousand tons, the probable velocity of fall, and the relative lightness of a ship's structure. A model of that ship one meter long would have had hull plates about as thick as aluminum foil. Obviously the drag of the water slowed the fall and the soft mud cushioned the impact to save this recently sunk ship from destruction just as it must have saved the old ones.

The question of how well the wood fibers have survived and how much strength they have left is more difficult. Evidence cited in a previous chapter shows that in some cold areas wood held undersea for many years retains most of its strength. The fact that it was possible to salvage the *Wasa* intact after three hundred years below the surface of Stockholm Harbor is an indication of the possibilities. Another piece of evidence is the generally good condition of old wood found in reducing environments. It will be black and slimy on the outside from sulphides and anaerobic bacteria, but the inside will probably retain much of its strength. These examples are not really adequate evidence, but they are encouraging. They give us reason to believe that in some environments ships will retain their shape and much of their strength even after thousands of years under water.

Now we can consider how to deal with an ancient undecked ship sitting upright on the bottom that retains at least half of its original strength, after its cargo has been removed by the remote manipulators. The hull of the hundred-ton merchantman used in the previous calculations would weigh about thirty-five tons in air (without ballast) but very little underwater. The problem is not so much the weight that must be raised but how to get a firm grip on the old hull without cracking it or crushing the softened wood.

One should have no illusions about the difficulties; under the best of conditions it will not be easy to raise a complete hull in a single lift. Even new ships cannot be picked up except from beneath in a carefully operated dry dock. Therefore we must design a structure that can get beneath the old ship and raise it by exerting upward pressure at a great many lift points simultaneously. In a dry dock, this is done by means of a series of blocks set at closely spaced intervals, each of which is pulled tightly against the hull to take an approximately equal amount of weight. When the lift is made, these blocks form a sort of fitted intermittent mold; the hull need only be strong enough to support itself between blocks.

In the deep-sea lift of an old hull, we must use the equivalent of a series of closely spaced blocks, because we will not know much about the strength of the wood. If the contact points are too widely spaced, the result could be like raising a rake through Jell-O. However, by using blocks spaced very close together and by fitting them or their padding to the hull, a delicate lift can be made. The questions then become: What should the blocks or contacts be made of? How are they inserted beneath the ship? How does the salvage ship exert force upward on them?

One possible solution is to freeze the bottom mud or water into a solid block of material and raise the block intact. This has the advantage of holding everything in its proper position and maintaining equal stresses throughout the hull. Unfortunately the amount of power required to freeze such a block and keep it frozen as it is brought to the surface and moved ashore is so large that this is a very impractical idea. One quick calculation and we abandoned this scheme.

Another round of design sketches, based on an idea suggested by Ted Mangles, a mechanical design engineer employed by Ocean Science and Engineering, Inc., called for a sort of upside-down dry dock. Something like an ordinary dry dock, this device would have wing walls along the sides (plus similar end walls) into which air could be pumped for flotation or water admitted to make it sink. The top side would be a rigid, covered structure to which the drill pipe would be attached and the open bottom could be closed by moving into place a belt of interlocking metal strips something like the top of a roll-top desk. In use, the procedure would be to hang this device beneath the *Alcoa Seaprobe* on cables, attach the drill pipe, and lower away. The upside-down dock would be carefully landed on the bottom over and around the hull to be salvaged. The wing walls would be jetted down into the mud, after which the metal roll-top plates would be closed beneath the old ship by pulling them with cables through mud liquefied by jets. The ancient hull would still be sitting on the original mud, but now it would be completely inside the dock.

A combination of air in the wing walls and lift by the *Alcoa Seaprobe*'s pipe would be used to raise the neatly packaged ancient ship to just beneath the recovery ship. While hanging there, the dry dock would be slowly moved into shallow water and set down on the bottom. The *Alcoa Seaprobe* would then move away and the dock could be floated. Now the entirely enclosed dock would be much like a covered barge and would be towed to its destination. Once there, divers could work inside the dock studying the old ship, and chemical preservatives could be added to keep the wooden hull's condition unchanged. Unfortunately it turned out to be very difficult to reduce this seemingly good idea to a practical design with reasonable costs. However, one of the most difficult problems was solved when Ed Horton devised a very clever way of injecting large quantities of air at great depths to give the dock the required flotation. Perhaps, for some special circumstance, a modification of this scheme will be useful.

Finally I decided that the best method for recovering ancient ships would be the most simple and direct. We would reach down and around the hull into the mud beneath, using a large set of tongs made of steel and actuated by a hydraulic system. These "super tongs" would be able to encompass an entire small ship or part of a large one by surrounding a space about ten meters (thirty-two feet) in diameter and twelve meters (forty feet) long. In other words, we would raise large objects about the same way the TVSS raised small ones. Weight, lifting power, and cost would all increase greatly, but they would remain within the realm of reason. Much larger and heavier vessels could be raised if the sizes of all the equipment, including the salvage ship, were enlarged.

The super tongs can do the most important thing; that is, they can close and latch in the mud beneath the old ship to form an absolutely rigid structure. As Figure 17 shows, they have three (or more) double tines that can operate independently. These broad tines—probably extended sidewise with plates and screens to give more bearing area in a final operational version—will support the mud that forms a soft cradle beneath the hulk. Much of the mud between ship and tongs will be brought up with the hull, still cushioning it as it has for thousands of years. In fact, the mud will be the principal weight raised; the waterlogged wood will weigh very little under water.

The tongs are of such great size and weight that they must be supplied with their own flotation so they do not add to the ship's lift burden and so they can be handled on the surface and towed to the site. When the tongs are to be lowered for a pickup, they are brought alongside the *Alcoa Seaprobe* and their buoyancy tanks flooded sufficiently so they barely sink; then they are slung beneath the ship on cables. Once the tongs are centered beneath the well, the pipe is attached, the slings released, and they are lowered away. As with the other bottom devices, they are equipped with lights and television cameras so that the operators on the ship can determine them to be precisely centered over the wreck with the tines all open. Finally, they will be slowly lowered the last few meters and the tines will be carefully closed around the wooden hulk. The illustration shows how three sets of independently operated tine pairs are hinged to a single large beam. The tines are opened and closed by pairs of hydraulic cylinders that act against articulated hinge plates in such a way that, as they close, increasingly greater force is applied at the tips. Just before complete closure, the penetrating power of each of the six double tine tips is about ten metric tons. This should be sufficient to penetrate the mud beneath an old ship and close tightly. When all are closed and locked in position, the lifting process will begin with a slow application of upward pull by the pipe accompanied by water jets discharging from the tines beneath the ship to break any suctional hold that the bottom may have.

In Figure 17, the tongs are shown closed about a small, open trading ship of 1000 B.C. whose dimensions are about eighteen meters long and seven meters beam (sixty by twenty-two feet). A ship of this size is well within the capacity of the super tongs and of *Alcoa Seaprobe*. This sketch illustrates one of the author's ideas for lifting ancient ships or other, similar-shaped large and heavy objects from deep water. Obviously, after a wreck has been found that is worthy of being raised, this design would be modified somewhat to fit the specific wreck's shape, size, weight, and estimated strength. As pointed out before, each step in the operation must be tailored to fit the circumstances that confront the searcher-salvor.

Finally, having raised the tongs and hulk to a position just below the ship, where the burden can be inspected by divers and where strengthening members can be added and the whole ship surrounded by nets to help hold it together, the *Alcoa Seaprobe* would move very slowly into shallow water. There it would set the tongs and ship down on the sea floor and move to one side. When the *Alcoa Seaprobe* is clear of the site, archaeological divers could go to work clearing the remaining mud, ballast, and artifacts from the ship to further lighten it. The mud supporting the hulk would be carefully removed and replaced with dry-dock blocks and wooden shims. Finally a structural framework would be added where necessary to support the ancient ship for its final move.

If the ancient ship the archaeologists wish to raise is too large to bring up in one piece, it will have to be cut into sections of manageable size. This might mean sawing it in two by means of a hydraulically powered chain saw after the cargo and ballast have been removed. For a long, slender warship such as a trireme this rather drastic step probably would be necessary. Or perhaps a pair of special trusses with flotation distributed along their length could be attached to the hull.

How one should proceed with a completely decked ship in good condition that is still loaded with cargo would, again, depend on the details of that ship. Since none has ever been found, obviously such a hull would be very valuable. Except for a very small vessel that could be raised intact, one would have to remove the decking somehow, because it would be necessary to get into

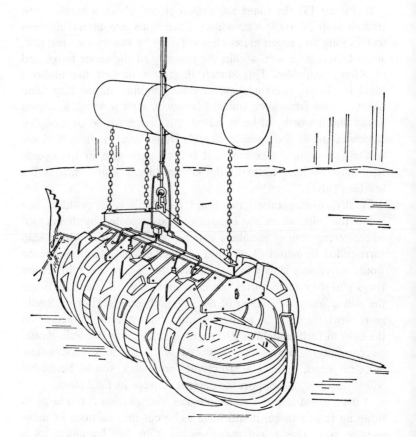

Figure 17. **The Super Tongs**

This is the author's conception of how a triple pair of independently operated tines might be closed beneath a small ship hull to seize and lift it in one piece. The pontoons above are used to float the tongs at the surface and to reduce their weight at depth. The entire device would be lowered and operated from *Alcoa Seaprobe.*

the hull and salvage the cargo and ballast before attempting to raise the ship. When this problem actually arises, doubtless the expedition leader will think of a reasonable solution that fits the situation.

Some archaeologists may recoil from the idea of cutting up a ship to salvage it; however, if it is possible to recover an ancient ship in good condition (except for a few clean saw cuts), this seems to me to be preferable to leaving it on the sea floor or carefully preserving, plank by plank, a poor hull from shallow water that must be reassembled like a giant jig-saw puzzle.

Now for the final move. With the raised hull safe in shallow water, a museum barge would be brought to the site. This barge would be a large, rectangular vessel containing a tank, full of water, large enough to hold the wreck. At this time, a high-lift-capacity marine derrick of the type that is available in many large harbors would be brought in to lift the hulk, still in the tongs but now surrounded by a rigid cradle, from the sea into the tank on the barge. Then the tongs would be released and removed, leaving the ship resting on dry-dock blocks in its new tank.

At last the ancient ship hull is in a position to be worked on by archaeologists. In this quiet, controlled environment, they can study the details and do whatever reconstruction is necessary for public viewing. This pool-on-a-barge will require a cover or baffles at the water surface to prevent sloshing and a roof overhead to keep out light that permits algae to grow. Appropriate chemicals to kill bacteria and inhibit decay would also be added.

Now, properly lighted in its underwater museum and equipped with dozens of viewing ports, this ship can be expected to attract the general public as well as the scholars—the natives as well as the tourists. The museum barge could be moved from one port to another as a traveling exhibit showing technological progress at sea and an example of international co-operation in the classical arts.

After recovery from the deep-sea floor, these works of the ancients, including the important fragments that illuminate the development of civilization, belong in museums, where they can be seen and studied by all interested persons. The question of which mu-

Figure 18. **A Floating Museum**

  One way to maintain an ancient hulk in good condition is to keep it submerged in chemically treated fresh water. If a hulk were brought up
largely intact by the super tongs, it might be set directly in a pool on a
barge. There archaeologists could work at restoring it while being observed by interested persons through portholes. As with the other ideas
sketched, this one needs careful thought before a final design is decided
on.

seum and the circumstances of how the treasures get there may be
the subject of some discussion.

  Arguments may arise from the conflicts between national desire
to exhibit the treasures of the past and the cost of building the facilities to do so. Nearly every country already has ample archaeological material from within its own boundaries to display if the
money were available for construction and upkeep of museum facilities. For material coming from well offshore in international
waters it is not so clear who should display it. Although it may be
possible to determine the wrecked ship's country of origin, it is
virtually certain that nation no longer exists. Who, then, except
the salvor is logically responsible for its preservation and disposition?

  An international museum run by the United Nations is a possibility, but many great museums already are international in the sense that they display ancient artifacts from many parts of the world. Eventually perhaps a multinational museum of ancient shipping can be created, but probably the most practical answer for the present is that the finds should be displayed where there is enough interest to pay for the facilities and their upkeep. The most logical place would seem to be a Mediterranean or Black Sea shipping center. However, any city that is convenient to international transportation might do as well.

If the money can be found to finance a new wing on an existing museum, to develop exhibits and to pay curators, does it matter where in the world the material is shown? The logic would be the same as that used to move and rebuild Egyptian temples about to be flooded by the Nile as it rose behind the Aswan High Dam. The temples were given to places that wanted them and could give them good homes. This certainly meets the grand objective of protecting the cultural heritage of mankind.

After an artifact or ship has been studied for itself and relative to its surroundings; after it has been measured, photographed, and become the subject of a scientific document; then it should be placed where it can be best appreciated. This will often be a museum near the site of the find, or, in the case of unusually valuable and unique treasures found in territorial waters, the appropriate national museum.

There are wealthy persons who are willing to sponsor archaeological expeditions to find and properly excavate ancient ships; should they not have the right to have a few of the pieces that are found in their private museums for the balance of their lifetime? After they die, the pieces would revert to public exhibition halls much as great paintings and other fine art pieces do. Does it make any difference now that many of the great statues of antiquity in the Louvre or the Metropolitan Museum once spent a few years in someone's palace or private collection?

I think not. The possibility of directly reimbursing a man with artistic pleasure in return for his financial contributions would greatly aid the financing of archaeological expeditions. Of course the source of funds must not be permitted to endanger the quality of the archaeological work or the judgment of the scientists involved. Most of the materials found would be of little personal interest; some items would be so rare and valuable or require such careful restoration and handling that they would be more nuisance than value to a private party. But it would make sense to allow a financial backer to proudly display a few special objects, already marked with the catalog numbers of their future museum, along with his personal collection. This kind of arrangement would be helpful to the world's archaeologists and museums. Especially when one considers the huge volume of unlooked-at, unavailable, and unloved material now gathering dust in museum basements and warehouses waiting for some hypothetical researcher of the future to show interest. In some cases public-museum storage facilities have proved not to be safe, the materials they hold often being as subject to flood, fire, and general deterioration as in any private museum.

Disposition depends of course on who owns the wreck and the material brought up; this requires an understanding of certain legal and political matters that are discussed in Appendix 1.

The important thing is to find, recover, and study the ancient ships and their cargoes. Previous chapters have described what ancient ships were like, what cargoes they carried, why ships are down, how they would be preserved by bottom conditions, and how one goes about searching and salvaging ancient objects from items as small as swords to those as large as complete ships. Finally we must consider exactly how to begin with the first steps that will reduce this new archaeological capability to practice in Mediterranean waters.

CHAPTER XII

Plans for the First
Deep Search

Now it is time to be specific about a program of sea operations. One begins by making a detailed plan that describes, with as much precision as possible, when, where, who, and how. So far this book has covered only the why of deep archaeology, the statistics of ship losses in various locations, and a description of the available tools. We have developed a good background in the history and oceanography of the Mediterranean; we know that virtually all the required equipment is already in existence and has undergone successful trials at sea of similar salvage jobs; we are intellectually prepared. But these things are largely theoretical; the proof that the ideas expressed here are good ones can come only from actually finding and salvaging very old ships.

A plan should describe the organization; the personnel; specific sites to be studied; political arrangements required; budget estimates; means of financing; ship schedules; mobilization and operating program; arrangements for cataloguing, identifying, preserving, and disposing of the materials recovered; target dates for various accomplishments; and contingency preparations.

It is still a little too early to announce publicly all the above details. Some of the plan has not yet been made or solidified; other parts are best kept confidential until financial commitments are set and arrangements made with foreign states. However, the following skeleton outline of a plan will answer many questions.

An archaeological expedition, particularly one intending to work with new and previously untried techniques, needs classical respectability. It must operate under the aegis of some highly reputable and credible organization. In this case the endeavors we wish to pursue are unusual, highly specialized, and rather expensive; they do not fit neatly under any existing organization, so a new one is being formed under one of the great universities of California. The Institute of Marine Archaeology will be a not-for-profit group under the university foundation, with faculty appointments for senior staff members.

The staff will be made up of a combination of permanent members who will be concerned full time with sea operations and archaeological work, faculty members with joint appointments, and students—both graduate and undergraduate. We expect to have no problem finding very-high-quality personnel to volunteer for duty aboard the search/recovery ships and in the archaeological laboratory. In fact, almost everyone who has heard this proposal has offered or even begged to come along in any capacity. Not only archaeologists, but medical doctors, lawyers, businessmen, engineers, and secretaries are eager to participate. This institute will develop associations with other archaeological institutes and universities interested in these matters, both in the United States and abroad. The people on shipboard are expected to be determined, well-trained, hard-working, and co-operative.

A major part of the operational plan depends upon the specific sites to be examined. First, site-selection criteria are established. Obviously, on the initial attempt it is important to maximize the chance of success. Eventually, it will be possible to explore waters that are very broad and deep, such as the Black Sea, where the chance of finding a ship is relatively low but where whatever is found will be in excellent condition. But in the beginning it is sensible to work where there is an almost certain chance of finding interesting ships in any condition and attracting interest to the project. Probably this means relatively shallow water (to three hundred meters, or a thousand feet) in restricted waterways where there was considerable ship traffic (on a main trade route) and a likelihood of sinkings due to sudden violent weather or attack by pirates. There is not enough information about any specific ancient sinking to warrant a search for that ship. Of course it would be possible to go back to Antikythera for the deep part of that wreck or to try to find again the statue-bearing hulk off Cape Artemision, but there are new and better opportunities ahead of us. The concept we are pursuing is based on the statistical chances of encountering old wrecks; our plan is to search areas of high probability.

The availability of funds governs the choice of the ship and equipment, and this, in turn, influences the choice of site. The *Alcoa Seaprobe* is certainly the best ship in the world for this kind of work, but it is expensive and is not absolutely necessary in water depths of a thousand feet or less. The offshore supply boat rigged with TVSS equipment will not be quite as nice an archaeologists' platform, but it is capable of proving the concept and finding old ships. It is to be hoped that after early successes we will advance to *Alcoa Seaprobe.*

Another matter to be considered in site selection is the legal situation (we must stay twelve miles offshore or outside a country's territorial waters). An alternative is to make appropriate political arrangements with nearby countries so that the expedition can work either inside or outside the sea area they control. If the local country is involved, presumably the finds would be divided with it in some equitable fashion. The advantages of having such arrangements are that possibly better sites can be chosen, local ports can be used with a minimum of red tape, local scientists and archaeologists with especially appropriate backgrounds can be employed, and the general atmosphere will be somewhat happier.

Based on the above reasoning and qualifications, I have selected the following four sites as having top priority for initial search with a small ship:

1. The Sea of Marmara to depths of a thousand feet along the main ship route between the Bosporus and the Dardanelles in an area where the dissolved oxygen content of the water is very low.

2. Several narrow passes between Greek islands, along the old

trade routes, look very promising. Exactly which ones should be searched depends on further study of the velocity of the currents and the nature of the bottom. For example, the passes between Evvoia and Andros, Kea and Kithnos, Kithera and Cape Malea, or Rhodes and the Turkish mainland.

3. Adventure Bank, along the shortest crossing between Sicily and Tunis, on the old sea road between Carthage and other Phoenician colonies. Also the site of Rome-Carthage traffic and clashes.

4. The sea around Malta, including the shallow Malta Channel to the north. Nearly every Mediterranean power for the past five thousand years has overrun Malta, and doubtless many left a few of their ships behind on the bottom. Minoans, Egyptians, Phoenicians, Romans, Arabs, and Turks influenced its history—which was already old with neolithic works when the first of them arrived. The wrecks must be there.

Now we come to scheduling and budgeting. This version is of course a rough approximation because many points remain to be decided, but it can serve as a guide. The ship is a major item. It may be possible to mobilize the equivalent of a 120-foot supply boat in the Mediterranean. If so some of the very substantial costs of mobilizing the ship from America can be saved (at twelve knots, or 288 miles a day, the time from the U. S. East Coast to Malta will be about two weeks). In addition, one must allow another two weeks for the return voyage, plus about two weeks for fueling, final outfitting, and crew rest. Thus a total of about six weeks of non-searching time. If a suitable ship can be found in the Mediterranean, about half of that time can be saved but the costs and problems of bringing in search/recovery equipment and getting it through customs and set up in operating fashion cancel much of the advantage.

A suitable steel ship with diesel engines (described in Chapter IX) and all the necessary equipment for careful navigation, setting buoys, anchoring in a thousand feet of water, operating the TVSS, accommodating the scientists properly, and riding out heavy weather without danger is not easy to charter outside the United States. The estimated cost of such a vessel, complete in all respects, with crew, fuel, and handling gear, will be about a thousand dollars a day, or $120,000 for the four months of reasonably good weather (June, July, August, and September). Since we expect to use six weeks in mobilization/demobilization, this leaves about ten weeks for search/recovery operations in the forward area. The working time can be extended if the weather remains good.

Special-equipment costs come next, the TVSS and side-looking sonar (both complete in all respects with winches, monitors, recorders, spare parts, troubleshooting equipment, etc.) initially cost around $150,000. However, since some of this equipment is already in existence and available slightly used, $100,000 will be budgeted.

Then there is a lot of miscellaneous equipment, including buoys, anchors, lines, duster, lifting baskets, and storage tanks, that will cost an estimated $15,000.

Some people will travel on the ship, but others will fly out and join the expedition at a round-trip cost of about $800 each, or $6,400 for eight persons. Salaries of six staff members during the planning, conduct, and reporting on the expedition will be about $60,000. Then there are travel and communications costs inside the United States and many small, miscellaneous items. Finally we get to a modest contingency item, commonly known as OSIF (for Oh Shucks, I Forgot) of $15,000 and university foundation overhead of 20 per cent on some of the above costs of about $25,000.

Thus the total cost of such an expedition adds up to about $341,000 for ten productive weeks at sea. Since, much of the time, the work goes on twenty-four hours a day, the actual operating time is about equivalent to twenty weeks of a land expedition. There are ways to reduce the costs somewhat, such as using a less expensive vessel to search with the side-looking sonar before the salvage ship arrives, but one must acknowledge that deep-sea expeditions are expensive. A second season's work, with the main equipment already purchased, would be about $230,000.

The work just budgeted is for the first preliminary expedition, which we expect to mount in the summer of 1976 or 1977. Many things remain to be done before that time that will influence the schedule. The organization must be completed and a staff engaged; detailed planning must be done; arrangements with governments and universities overseas must be made; and the institute and the project must be financed.

As with most other things in this world, the financing must come first so that the wherewithal exists to hire and plan and operate. There are a number of possible sources of funds. These include the university itself, the federal government via the National Foundation for the Humanities or the National Science Foundation, and private foundations. Because this is a glamorous and exciting project with a very good chance of making a real break-through in archaeology and history, wealthy individuals with classical tastes can be expected to help finance some of the work. Whoever does has a good chance of becoming a modern Lord Carnarvon, who sponsored Howard Carter in the finding of Tutankhamen's tomb, or Alexander Benaki, who financed the salvage of the great bronze statues at Cape Artemision. Much remains to be discovered in the sea, and the methods described here have the best chance of success.

It is not possible to see into the future in great detail. I have always thought that Thomas Carlyle wisely described the best route when he said, "Go as far as you can see. Then you will be able to see further."

Epilogue

Once upon a time the gods of the ancient world met in council atop Mount Olympus to decide how their handiwork could best be preserved for those that would come afterward.

"We must be sure that examples survive of the greatest expression of artistic genius," said one; "perhaps the best evidence would be bronze statues of ourselves," and he lowered his eyes modestly. Another spoke: "It would be best to preserve the body of a great king and all his treasures in a very dry climate; I have in mind Agamemnon or Tutankhamen."

Chac arose, his terrible headdress shimmering with rain: "We can keep our best treasure underwater in my sacred well at Chichén Itzá. It will be a hundred generations before anyone will discover a way to get to it." Then Thor leaned forward in his massive throne: "A ship is the best container, but let us keep it on land under a mound of earth, perhaps at Sutton Hoo or along the Great Fjord."

"Everyone knows that ice is the best way to preserve things," said Slav: "I can keep a whole family with all their servants and possessions in a special tomb in Siberia. It will last as long as the hairy mammoths I have there now." Vulcan exploded: "Ash is the better preservative. Soft, light, and dry, it will keep its secrets safe in a reasonable climate. Santorin or Vesuvius would give a perfect cover for an entire city."

Zeus, who spends his days watching over the broad blue sea from his cloudy temple and so is sometimes mistaken for Poseidon, listened thoughtfully to these diverse views. Then he threw a small thunderbolt to still the younger gods and spoke his decision. "My friends, your ideas are good ones and we should try them all. The future races of man will have a delightful time seeking the clues we leave in many diverse places and trying to decide what our world was like. However, I have an additional suggestion that will include all the kinds of treasures you have mentioned and a few more. In order to leave a continuing sample of all civilizations for the ones that come afterward, I hereby decree that one ship in ten will sink as it crosses my deepwater domain. The abyss will hold our treasures safe in its vault for thousands of years until mankind is ready for them. Don't you agree?"

The circle of gods nodded in approval.

APPENDIX 1

Legal Matters Related to Salvaging Deep Wrecks

The law of the sea is complicated and changing. Not all countries agree on the extent of jurisdiction that a coastal state has over the waters off its shores. Some states have signed the international agreement and some have not; others have retained the old limits, pending new agreements.

New ideas about the rights of nations in the ocean are being considered and passionately debated. One hundred and forty-five states were represented at the United Nations Seabed 1973 organizational meetings in New York; they reconvened for an eight-week working meeting in Caracas, Venezuela, in 1974, and they plan to gather again for meetings in Geneva and Vienna. It is to be hoped that the eventual result will be agreement between nations on territorial rights in the sea. Then order will prevail over the present uncertainties.

The discussion here is therefore subject to some change in the next few years, but it is possible to make a fairly good guess at the probable outcome. The main considerations of the countries involved are natural resources, military problems, and commercial routes; such items as scientific work and archaeology are far down the list in importance. The natural resources that are the topic of most intense debate are mainly the metal-containing nodules on the deep-sea floor, the petroleum products on the continental shelves, and fish in mid-water. Every nation wants a share of these, and many of the developing countries view with suspicion any kind of scientific work or exploration on the grounds that it will somehow lead to exploitation in which they will not participate.

After imperial Rome's control of the Mediterranean faded, the seas were free to the strong. Sailors sailed where they wished and were responsible for their own defense against attack by pirates or ships of an unfriendly state. But in the 1500s, as navigators and explorers began to push out into distant seas, the Pope divided the unknown world between Spain and Portugal to keep these Catholic countries from too violent a competition. Generally, Spain got the Western Hemisphere, Portugal the Eastern. But the Dutch, English, and French were not far behind in claiming their rights; what they claimed was the "freedom of the seas." All fought repeatedly over this issue, but in time freedom became accepted as international doctrine.

This doctrine is still in use, particularly with respect to navigation, overflight, commerce, and science. However, for other matters it is being reconsidered. The subject of sea rights had been dormant for some time when, in 1945, President Harry Truman claimed for the United States all the resources on its adjacent shelf out to a water depth of two hundred meters. Although the United States still claimed only three miles of the ocean surface, with that proclamation a very much larger area of the ocean floor was added. Obviously, in order to work on the bottom far offshore, one must control the surface at that spot, and so the debate began. Now other states used Truman's action to justify their claims for more extensive jurisdiction. For example, Brazil, Ecuador, and Peru claim two-hundred-mile territorial waters; for fishing rights, Chile claims two hundred miles, Morocco seventy, and Iceland fifty.

Marine artifacts are considered to be abandoned property under both civil and common law. But property in a strict legal sense does not mean a physical object; rather, it is the exclusive right to possess and dispose of the object. Therefore an abandoned and unfound object does not legally have the status of "property." Only after it is found and comes into someone's possession does a submerged object become abandoned property. If there is no specific titleholder and if the object is found outside the limit claimed by any state, title to the property "vests in the person who first reduces it to possession."

Property is abandoned when it is totally deserted and absolutely relinquished by the former owner. This may occur when the owner specifically casts the property away or leaves it behind or, after an unintentional loss, gives up any attempt to reclaim it. Clearly, ancient wrecks outside the territorial water and legislative reach of any state are abandoned property. The question then becomes: what are the territorial waters of a coastal state and how far does its jurisdiction extend?

The most fundamental source of information on existing laws is the First Law of the Sea Convention, which resulted from the Geneva Conference of 1958. The conventions that were agreed upon for the most part codified what was already generally accepted as peacetime laws. They began by designating five geographical-legal zones, called as follows: internal waters, territorial seas, contiguous zone, high seas, and continental shelf.

For the following discussion of these areas and of the present legal position of various countries, this chapter draws heavily on the work of

David P. Stang, a staff man for the U. S. Senate Committee on Interior and Insular Affairs; on H. Crane Miller's short book on *International Law and Marine Archaeology* (he was also once a Senate staffer and counsel to the Oceans and Atmosphere Subcommittee); and on "Marine Archaeology and International Law," by Howard Shore, in the *San Diego Law Review*. Their thoroughly referenced papers quoted here largely used the wording of the original conventions.

In deciding the extent of a state's claims to areas of the sea, one begins by drawing a base line on a chart so that there is a precise place from which to measure. Normally this is the low-water line along a coast marked on large-scale charts that are officially recognized by the coastal state. Where the coast is deeply indented or if there is a fringe of islands in the immediate vicinity, straight base lines between promontories may be drawn, but these must not depart to any appreciable extent from the general direction of the coast. In drawing these base lines, account may be taken of economic interests peculiar to the region but on no account shall they be applied in such a manner as to infringe on the territorial seas of another state. Finally, the coastal state must clearly indicate its straight base lines on charts to which due publicity must be given.

Waters on the landward side of the base line are called "internal." They include small bays, harbors, river mouths, and waters on the landward side of islands situated along the base line. These waters are legally just like the state's land mass in the sense that it exercises complete sovereignty over them and can exclude foreign ships.

The "territorial sea" is a belt of sea adjacent to a state's coast, the outer limit of which is a line equidistant from the base line. The Geneva conventions did not specify the width of the territorial sea in nautical miles; as a result, there have been many international arguments on the proper width.

At present, seventy coastal states out of one hundred and twenty claim a territorial sea breadth of twelve miles, and twelve states claim up to two hundred miles. The three-mile width, now claimed mainly by the United States and Commonwealth countries, was established in the 1600s by a pragmatic Dutch jurist who decided that the law could be enforced to the distance reached with a cannon ball from shore. In the age of transoceanic missiles, the cannon-ball rule must be replaced by modern laws.

By September 1972, the U. S. Department of State had modified its previous position calling for a three-mile limit and submitted to the ninety-one-member U. N. Seabed Committee draft treaty articles that provide that (1) the territorial sea would be fixed at a maximum breadth of twelve nautical miles and (2) there would be free transit through and over international straits. On the subject of seabed resources, the United States proposed to limit all national claims to the seabed to an area where the depth is less than two hundred meters, and that international machinery be set up to license exploration and exploitation beyond that depth.

The United States entered the 1973 conference willing to agree to broad coastal-state economic jurisdiction beyond the territorial sea as part of an over-all law-of-the-sea settlement if international standards are established. These standards would include treaty articles that would prevent unreasonable interference with other uses of the ocean, protect against pollution, safeguard maritime investments, provide for compulsory settlement of disputes, and call for revenue-sharing of returns from deep-ocean resources.

Innocent passage of foreign ships is permitted in territorial waters without the consent of the coastal state concerned; that is, ships may pass through the zone going to or coming from internal waters. These ships may stop and anchor, but their right to search for and recover sunken property would be subject to the laws of the coastal state. Most marine archaeology done to date has been well within these territorial waters and so has properly been under the jurisdiction of the adjacent state.

Just outside the territorial sea is the "contiguous zone," which extends twelve miles from the base line out into the high seas. In this zone the coastal state may exercise the control necessary to prevent or punish infringements of its customs, immigration, or pollution regulations within its territorial zone. It is specifically not intended for security, on the ground that the state's inherent right of self-defense provides an adequate basis for taking action.

No test of the legality of recovering sunken property in the contiguous zone without the permission of the adjacent state is known to have been made. Because it is part of the high seas, every state has the right to operate there under its own flag. On the other hand, the coastal state may wish to exercise some control over the activities of ships of other nations who are infringing in some way on its customs, fiscal, immigration, or sanitary regulations. Until this is settled, naval might, driven by political pressures, will govern. Presumably, when the twelve-mile territorial sea is finally agreed upon, the contiguous zone will vanish.

The two remaining areas, "high seas" and "continental shelf," also begin at the outer edge of the territorial sea. The high seas means all parts of the sea that are not included in the territorial sea or the internal waters of any state. In all areas of the unrestricted high seas out-side any contiguous zone, a vessel may generally be said to have the right to conduct scientific research (including archaeological work) and to search for and recover sunken property. The exception to this rule may be based on claims by the coastal state related to the conti-nental shelf. All states, coastal or not, have the right to operate ships on the high seas under their own flags; private vessels have a similar right deriving from the right of the country whose flag they fly.

The right of states to use the unrestricted high seas is almost unlim-ited as long as no other state's peace and security are threatened. It is conceivable that there could be some circumstances involving the ac-tivities of a private salvage operation conducted on the high seas ad-jacent to a state that would appear to pose a threat to that state's security and thus cause a reaction, but this seems unlikely.

The "continental shelf" refers to the seabed and subsoil of the sub-marine areas adjacent to the coast but outside the territorial sea to a depth of two hundred meters or "beyond that limit to where the depth of the superadjacent water admits of the exploration of the natural resources of the said area." This raises some interesting legal questions, such as: What constitutes exploitability? If the depth of the superad-jacent water is not limiting, how deep can one go?

The purpose of the convention on the continental shelf is to give a coastal state the sovereign right to exploit its natural resources; how-ever, man-made sunken property can hardly be considered a natural resource. The rights of a coastal state over the continental shelf do not legally affect the waters above the shelf. However, the state may main-tain permanent installations such as fabricated steel towers for the ex-ploitation of its resources, surrounded by safety zones five hundred meters wide from which salvage may be excluded. There are also gen-eral rules that (1) exploration for scientific and archaeological pur-poses must not interfere with navigation and (2) the results are to be made freely available through the scientific literature.

Article 2 of the 1960 Convention on the Continental Shelf of the Law of the Sea Conference at Geneva defined the rights of states on the continental shelves and described natural resources as "the min-eral and other non-living resources of the seabed and subsoil together with living organisms belonging to sedimentary species, that is, organ-isms which, at the harvestable stage, are immobile on or under the seabed, or are unable to move except in constant physical contact with the seabed."

The International Law Commission, in its report covering the eighth session, made these comments on the subject: "It is clearly understood that the rights in question do not cover objects such as wrecked ships and their cargoes (including bullion) lying on the seabed or covered, by the sand of the subsoil." Thus it appears, according to H. Crane Miller, that the proposed convention would not change the law of salvage, which applies to wrecks and cargoes, including bullion, all of which are abandoned property, even though the recovery of such wrecks entails physical contact with the seabed and removal of sand or other materials to reach the wreck.

Article 5 of the Convention on the Continental Shelf further says: "The consent of the coastal State shall be obtained in respect of any research concerning the continental shelf and undertaken there. Nevertheless, the coastal State shall not normally withhold its consent if the request is submitted by a qualified institution with a view to purely scientific research into the physical or biological characteristics of the continental shelf, subject to the proviso that the coastal State shall have the right, if it so desires, to participate or to be represented in the research, and that in any event, the results shall be published."

The United Nations 25th General Assembly, in 1970, passed a "legal principles" resolution that asserts there is an area of seabed beyond the limits of national jurisdiction that no nation may appropriate or exercise sovereign rights on. This implies that the "freedom of the seas" doctrine still applies. Thus, in the opinion of leading maritime experts, there is freedom to conduct scientific research and salvage operations on the deep seabed.

In most of these international discussions, marine archaeology is not specifically mentioned as an agenda item, but the convention articles that deal with "science" express approximately equivalent views. However, in the 1971 Law of the Sea meetings, the Greek representative reminded the others that his delegation had proposed the inclusion of an agenda item entitled "Archaeological and Historical Treasures of the Sea Bed and the Ocean Floor Beyond the Limits of National Jurisdiction." "Mankind," he said, "should be given the opportunity of enjoying the rich archaeological and historical treasures of the seabed which it should be one of the functions of the international machinery to protect."

The U. N. Seabed Committee is now trying to provide a new law of the sea that will translate the concept "common heritage of mankind" into specific legal arrangements. It is first necessary to agree on the area to which the common-heritage concept applies. The most likely final compromise will be a twelve-mile-wide territorial sea and free transit through all straits guaranteed by treaty. Between twelve and two hundred miles, there would be a "resource zone," with states being given limited jurisdiction for specific purposes such as fisheries and mineral-resource management. This zone between twelve and two hundred miles includes nearly 30 per cent of the world ocean and all of the Mediterranean and Black seas that are of interest to the deepwater archaeologist.

If these conventions do prevail and are ratified, there will be an effective twelve-mile limit within which the Mediterranean and Black sea countries will have effective control over wrecks and artifacts on the bottom. Outside that area it is evident only a highly developed and expensive technology such as that proposed here will be likely to find old wrecks and salvage them. If this work is not sponsored by one of the adjacent countries, that is hardly a reason to believe that it will be less competently done and reported by citizens of another country.

Much of the great archaeological work in Mediterranean lands in the past has been done by German, French, and British workers. Considerable undersea archaeology has been done by French, Greek, and Italian divers (not necessarily off the shores of their own countries) and by Americans who have generously donated time and money to the cause of understanding ancient ships and civilizations. Some of the most important finds have been made by dedicated but non-trained archaeologists. Mainly, these men have left their finds behind for local museums, sometimes in contrast to the local divers, who have been known to smuggle ancient objects out of the country for private sale.

Often the scientific credentials of foreign archaeological teams have been less carefully scrutinized than their finances or their political leanings.

Undersea archaeology is legally and conceptually quite different from undersea mining or oil drilling. It is done only by intensely interested individuals and is totally inappropriate for corporations whose purpose is profit. It attracts men who expect to work long, hard hours for very little pay and who are content to be rewarded with the minor glory that comes from new scientific or historic discoveries. They would rather be known as the finder of an important ancient wreck or historical fact than have the monetary return that would come from equivalent work in other fields. It is virtually certain that search-and-salvage operations, whatever they may be, will cost more than any likely monetary return. Archaeological expeditions following the ideas set forth here will not only be probing new depths for historical treasures but new areas of international interest.

This means that national prestige will sometimes be at stake. Even though archaeological finds are made well outside of any legally claimed sea boundary, the nearest state may feel that somehow these relate to its national history and wish to be involved. In any case, the archaeologist leader would be wise to invite qualified archaeologists of nearby countries to participate in his expedition and to report back to their countrymen on whatever happens. Then there would be no opportunity for rumors to start that suggest something valuable is being discovered and kept secret from the outside world.

In summary, the present laws of the sea permit archaeological salvage operations outside the twelve-mile limit off all Mediterranean countries, but it would be well to have friendly political arrangements before starting to work.

Table 7. **Territorial Seas Claimed by Mediterranean and Black Sea Countries Compared with the U.K. and the U.S.A. 1973 (after H. Crane Miller)**

	Width of Territorial sea	Fishing Limit
Albania	12	12
Algeria	12	12
Bulgaria	12	12
Cyprus	12	12
Egypt	12	12*
France	12	12
Greece	6	6
Israel	6	6
Italy	6	12
Lebanon	no legislation	6
Libya	12	12
Malta	6	6
Monaco	3	12
Morocco	12	70**
Spain	6	12
Syria	12	12*
Tunisia	6	12
Turkey	6 Mediterranean Sea	12
Turkey	12 Black Sea	12
U.S.S.R.	12	12
Yugoslavia	10	12
U.K.	3	12
U.S.A.	3	12

* Plus six miles "necessary supervision" zone
** Except six miles at Strait of Gibraltar

APPENDIX 2

The Metric System

A very large part of the world and virtually all Mediterranean countries use the metric system of weights and measurements because of the convenient interrelationship between distance, volume, mass, and temperature and the use of decimal steps. It has long been employed by American scientists and is slowly coming into general use.

This book uses the units of the original authors or charts from which the data were taken, and these are mostly metric. In some cases, the equivalent English units have been added for the reader's convenience. Meters are used for depths and distances. Since often these numbers are estimates or approximations, if one mentally multiplies by 3 to convert meters to feet the answer will not be far off.

A few of the more useful metric-English conversions are given below. All miles used in the text are nautical miles.

1 inch	=	2.54 centimeters		
1 foot	=	30.5 centimeters		
1 nautical mile	=	6,076 feet	=	1,852 meters
1 meter	=	3.28 feet		
1 kilometer	=	3,280 feet		
1 pound	=	.453 kilogram		
1 metric ton	=	1,000 kilograms		
1 kilogram	=	2.21 pounds		
1 liter	=	.265 gallon		
1 gallon	=	3.78 liters		

Temperature

Freezing (water)	=	0° Celsius (centigrade)	=	32° Fahrenheit
Boiling (water)	=	100° Celsius (centigrade)	=	212° Fahrenheit
Room temperature	=	22° Celsius (centigrade)	=	72° Fahrenheit

REFERENCES USED

Books

Bass, George (ed.). *A History of Seafaring Based on Underwater Archaeology.* Thames and Hudson, London, 1972.

Boardman, J. *The Greeks Overseas.* Penguin Books, Baltimore, 1964.

Bradford, Ernle. *The Mediterranean.* Hodder and Stoughton, London, 1971.

Brandon, S. G. F. (ed.). *Ancient Empires.* Weidenfeld & Nicolson, Italy, 1970.

Casson, Lionel. *The Ancient Mariners.* The Macmillan Company, New York, 1959.

————. *Ships and Seamanship in the Ancient World.* Princeton University Press, Princeton, N.J., 1971.

Culican, William. *The First Merchant Venturers.* McGraw-Hill, New York, 1966.

Denham, H. M. *The Aegean.* John Murray, London, 1963.

Flemming, Nicholas. *Cities in the Sea.* Doubleday, New York, 1971.

Frost, H. *Under the Mediterranean.* Routledge and Kegan Paul, London, 1963.

Gilley, W. *Narratives of Shipwrecks of the Royal Navy.* London, 1851.

Glob, P. V. *The Bog People.* Ballantine Books, New York, 1971.

Gores, Joseph. *Marine Salvage.* Doubleday, New York, 1971.

Heyden, A. A. M. van der; and H. H. Scullard. Atlas of the Classical World. Thomas Nelson and Sons, London, 1959.

Miller, H. Crane. *International Law and Marine Archaeology.* Academy of Applied Science, Belmont, Mass., 1973.

Rackl, H. Wolf. *Diving into the Past.* Charles Scribner's Sons, New York, 1968.

Rodgers, W. L. *Greek and Roman Naval Warfare.* U. S. Naval Institute, Annapolis, Md., 1964.

Throckmorton, Peter. *The Lost Ships.* Little, Brown & Co., Boston, 1964.

————. *Shipwrecks and Archaeology.* Atlantic-Little, Brown, New York, 1969.

Torr, Cecil. *Ancient Ships.* Argonaut, Inc., Publishers, Chicago, 1964.

Zenkevich, L. *Biology of the Seas of the U.S.S.R.* George Allen & Unwin, London, 1963.

Articles

Dixon, J. E.; J. Cann, and Colen Renfrew. "Obsidian and the Origins of Trade," *Scientific American,* March 1968, pp. 38–46.

Evans, J. W. "Marine Borer Activity in Test Boards Operated in the Newfoundland Area During 1967–68," Contribution No. 39 of Marine Sciences Research Laboratory, Memorial University of Newfoundland.

E. J. F. "Bronze," Encyclopaedia Britannica, Vol. 4, pp. 241–42, 1948.

Frazer, J. Z.; G. Arrhenius, *et al.* "Surface Sediment Distribution— Mediterranean Sea," Scripps Institution of Oceanography for the U. S. Navy, 1970.

Jannasch, H. W.; and C. O. Wirsen. "Deep-Sea Microorganisms: In Situ Response to Nutrient Enrichment," *Science,* May 11, 1973, pp. 641–43.

Kohlmeyer, Jan. "Deterioration of Wood by Marine Fungi in the Deep Sea," Special Technical Publication No. 445, pp. 20–30. North Carolina Institute of Marine Sciences.

Lancaster, Donald. "Electronic Metal Detectors," *Electronics World,* December 1966, pp. 39–42.

Meyer, Karl E. "The Plundered Past," *The New Yorker,* March 24, March 31, and April 7, 1973.

Muraoka, J. S. "Deep Ocean Biodeterioration of Materials—Six Months at 6000 Feet," U. S. Naval Civil Engineering Laboratory technical note N-1081, April 1970.

Price, Derek de Solla. "An Ancient Greek Computer," *Scientific American,* June 1959, pp. 60–67.

Ross, D. A.; E. T. Egens, and J. MacIlvaine. "Black Sea: Recent Sedimentary History," *Science,* October 9, 1970, pp. 163–65.

Shore, Howard H. "Marine Archaeology and International Law: Background and Some Suggestions," *The San Diego Law Review,* Vol. 9, No. 3, May 1972. The University of San Diego.

Stang, Phillip D. "International Law and Right of Access," a position paper done privately for ALCOA and Seafinders, Inc., 1971.

Stevenson, John. "Who Is to Control the Oceans?" *The International Lawyer,* Vol. 6, No. 3, July 1972, pp. 465–77.

Turner, Ruth D. "Some Results of Deep Water Testing," Annual Reports for 1965, The American Malacological Union, pp. 9–11.

———. "Wood Boring Bivalves, Opportunistic Species in the Deep Sea," *Science,* June 29, 1973, pp. 1377–79.

Wallace, B. L.; and W. A. Colleti. "Evaluation of Materials Exposed for One Year on a Deep Sea Array in the Tongue of the Ocean, Bahamas," Naval Research Laboratory report, 9–15 October 1970.

Index